THiNK

STUDENT'S BOOK 3A

B1+

Herbert Puchta, Jeff Stranks & Peter Lewis-Jones

CAMBRIDGE
UNIVERSITY PRESS

CONTENTS

Welcome p 4

A *let* and *allow*; Music; Verbs of perception; The big screen; Present perfect tenses; TV programmes

B Our endangered planet; Question tags; *So do I / Neither do I*; Accepting and refusing invitations; Party time; Indefinite pronouns; Arranging a party

C Feeling under the weather; Giving advice; Better or worse?; Comparisons

D Reported speech; Sequencing words; Asking for and offering help; IT problems; IT vocabulary; Passive tenses

	FUNCTIONS & SPEAKING	GRAMMAR	VOCABULARY
Unit 1 Life plans p 12	Complaining Role play: Complaining to a family member Talking about the future	Present tenses (review) Future tenses (review)	Making changes Life plans **WordWise**: Phrases with *up*
Unit 2 Hard times p 20	Talking about the past	Narrative tenses (review) *would* and *used to*	Descriptive verbs Time periods

	FUNCTIONS & SPEAKING	GRAMMAR	VOCABULARY
Unit 3 What's in a name? p 30	Giving advice Expressing obligation Giving recommendations, warnings and prohibitions	*(don't) have to / ought to / should(n't) / must* *had better (not)* *can('t) / must(n't)*	Making and selling Expressions with *name*
Unit 4 Dilemmas p 38	Apologising and accepting apologies Talking about hypothetical situations Expressing wishes	First and second conditional (review) Time conjunctions *wish* and *if only* Third conditional (review)	Being honest Making a decision **WordWise**: *now*

PRONUNCIATION	THINK	SKILLS	
Linking words with *up*	**Train to Think:** Reading between the lines **Self-esteem:** Life changes	Reading	Article: I miss my bad habits Article: For a better life … Photostory: What's up with Mia?
		Writing	An email about resolutions
		Listening	A conversation about famous people who started their careers late
Initial consonant clusters with /s/	**Train to Think:** Following an idea through a paragraph **Values:** Animal rights	Reading	Article: Events that shook the world Article: Family life in 17th-century Britain Culture: Where life is really hard
		Writing	A magazine article about a historical event
		Listening	A class presentation about animals being put on trial
Strong and weak forms: /ɒv/ and /əv/	**Train to Think:** Identifying the main topic of a paragraph **Self-esteem:** People and their names	Reading	Article: Brand names Article: Crazy names Fiction: *Wild Country* by Margaret Johnson
		Writing	A reply to a letter asking for advice
		Listening	A conversation about techniques for remembering names
Consonant–vowel word linking	**Train to Think:** Thinking of consequences **Values:** Doing the right thing	Reading	Quiz: What would YOU do? Article: The day Billy Ray's life changed forever Photostory: And the hole gets deeper!
		Writing	A diary entry about a dilemma
		Listening	A guessing game: Famous Wishes

WELCOME

A THAT'S ENTERTAINMENT!
let and *allow*

1 🔊 1.02 **Complete the conversation with the words. Then listen and check.**

~~looking~~ | allowed | makes | talent show | cross
songs | look | feel | sound | guitar | get | let

LISA Hey, Kim, what are you [0] *looking* at?

KIM My Science book. Can't you see I'm busy?

LISA I'm just asking. Sorry.

KIM No, I'm sorry. I don't [1]_____ great today.

LISA You don't [2]_____ very happy. What's the matter?

KIM My dad [3]_____ me so [4]_____ .

LISA That doesn't [5]_____ so good. Why?

KIM He says I'm not [6]_____ to be in the band.

LISA What?! So he won't allow you to play in the [7]_____ next week?

KIM No. He says no music until after my exams.

LISA But they don't finish for four weeks!

KIM I know. He wants me to study and forget about writing [8]_____ . He won't even [9]_____ me practise the [10]_____ .

LISA But you need some time to relax.

KIM I know. I [11]_____ so angry when I think about it. It just isn't fair.

2 🔊 1.02 **Listen again. Answer the questions.**

1 Why is Kim angry?

2 How long is it until the exams finish?

3 What does Lisa think about the situation?

4 Who do you agree with: Kim or her dad? Why?

3 **SPEAKING** **What do your parents allow you to do during exam time? What don't they let you do? Make lists. Then compare with a partner.**

Music

Sort the words into two groups. Label the groups. Then think of four more items for each one.

drums | classical | jazz | violin
guitar | pop | piano | rap

Verbs of perception

1 **Complete the sentences from the conversation with the correct forms of (*not*) *look*. Then match them with the rules.**

1 You _____ very happy.

2 Hey, Kim, what _____ at?

> **RULE:** We use verbs of perception (*look, smell, feel, taste*) …
>
> in the **present continuous** to talk about **actions**. ☐
>
> in the **present simple** to talk about **states**. ☐

2 **Complete the mini-dialogues with the correct forms of the verbs.**

1 taste

A What are you doing?

B I _____ the soup … It _____ great.

2 smell

A My socks _____ really bad!

B Then why _____ you _____ them?

3 feel

A Why _____ you _____ that jumper?

B Because it's so soft. I like the way it _____ .

3 **Work in pairs. Kim tries to persuade her dad to let her play in the talent show. Write a conversation of eight lines. Then read it out.**

The big screen

1 SPEAKING Work in pairs. For each type of film, think of an example that you have both seen.

action | animated | comedy | drama | horror | romantic comedy | science fiction | thriller

2 Read the article. What types of films does it mention?

3 Read the article again and mark the sentences T (true), F (false) or DS (doesn't say).

1 Chris Columbus's films are popular with 13–18-year-olds. ☐

2 Columbus started making films when he was 30. ☐

3 His films aren't popular with older people. ☐

4 Lots of people in Hollywood want Columbus to make films. ☐

5 He's never won an Oscar. ☐

4 SPEAKING Work in pairs. Think of your favourite film director and discuss these questions.

1 What films has this director made?

2 What do you like about his/her films?

Present perfect tenses

Complete the sentences. Use the present perfect simple or continuous form of the verbs and (circle) the correct words.

1 They _____ (play) *for / since* 87 minutes and neither side has scored yet.

2 I *yet / still* _____ (not watch) the final, so please don't tell me which singer won.

3 _____ you _____ (see) last night's show *still / yet*? Brad Pitt and Lady Gaga were guests.

4 The children _____ (sit) in front of the TV watching *SpongeBob for / since* they got up.

5 It's the funniest programme on TV. I _____ (not miss) an episode *still / yet*.

6 The Prime Minister _____ (say) the same thing *for / since* weeks now. No one believes him.

Behind the camera

Chris Columbus

A 12-year-old who gets left behind when his family go on holiday, a teenage magician fighting to save his world and the troubled son of a Greek god living in modern-day America: these are just three of the characters brought to life on the big screen by director Chris Columbus. With films such as *Home Alone*, *Harry Potter and the Chamber of Secrets* and *Percy Jackson and the Sea of Monsters*, Columbus has certainly shown that he knows how to get teenagers into the cinema.

Columbus has been making films for more than 30 years and has become one of the most successful film directors of all time. Since he directed his first film, *Adventures in Babysitting*, in 1987, Columbus has been involved in some of the biggest films as both a director and a producer.

But Columbus doesn't only make action films for the teenage market. He's also made a number of successful films for adults. Comedies such as *Mrs Doubtfire*, dramas such as *The Help* and science fiction films such as *Bicentennial Man* have all helped make Columbus one of Hollywood's most popular film-makers.

TV programmes

1 Work in pairs. Look at the sentences in the previous exercise. Match them with the types of TV programme.

talent show | sitcom | cartoon | sports programme | the news | chat show

2 Choose a type of TV programme from the list below. Write a sentence about it using the present perfect simple and/or continuous. Don't include the type of programme in your sentence!

drama series | game show | reality show | soap (opera)

I've been watching it for weeks, but no one has won the million-dollar prize yet.

3 SPEAKING Read out your sentence. Can the rest of the class guess the type of TV programme?

B TIME TO ACT
Our endangered planet

1 [SPEAKING] Work in pairs. Describe the photos. What problems do they show?

 A

 B

 C

2 [🔊 1.03] Listen to three conversations. Match them with the photos.

3 [🔊 1.03] Listen again. In which conversation do you hear these words? Write the number.

a rubbish ☐
b global warming ☐
c litter ☐
d pollution ☐
e fumes ☐
f smog ☐
g flooding ☐

Question tags

1 Complete these sentences from the recording with the question tags.

are they? | aren't they? | does it?
did they? | is it? | isn't it?
weren't they? | doesn't it?

1 I guess they're just lazy, _____
2 But it only takes a few people to spoil everything, _____
3 Yes, it's all those fumes from the factory, _____
4 They didn't ask us if we wanted it here, _____
5 Even if they do, it doesn't make our lives any better, _____
6 Hundreds of homes were damaged _____
7 And the politicians aren't really doing anything to help, _____
8 It isn't the sort of thing you'd expect to see here, _____

2 Complete the sentences with question tags.

1 You haven't told Ron, _____?
2 You're going to do something about it, _____?
3 It sounds quite dangerous, _____?
4 It didn't work, _____?
5 It won't be easy, _____?
6 She wrote to her local politician, _____?

So do I / Neither do I

1 Look at the questions and complete the answers with *so* or *neither*.

1 A I don't really believe in all that.
   B _____ do I.

2 A I think we should do something.
   B _____ do I.

2 [SPEAKING] Complete the sentences so that they are true for you and read them out. Agree (or disagree!) with your partner's sentences.

1 I really like _____
2 I don't like _____
3 I believe _____
4 I don't believe _____

Accepting and refusing invitations

1 [🔊 1.04] Put the sentences in order to make a conversation. Then listen and check.

1	SUE	Marco and I want to do something to help the flood victims.
	SUE	Yes – 20 km! <u>Want to join us?</u>
	SUE	<u>That's a shame.</u> But <u>you will</u> sponsor us, <u>won't you?</u>
	SUE	We're going to do a sponsored walk next Sunday.
	DEREK	<u>Of course I will.</u>
	DEREK	Are you going to walk a long way?
	DEREK	What are you going to do?
	DEREK	<u>I'd love to, but I can't.</u> I'm busy.

2 Work in pairs. Write a conversation using the <u>underlined</u> phrases from Exercise 1.

You and your friend are tired of all the rubbish in the street and have decided to do something about it. What are you going to do? Invite another friend to join you.

Party time

1 Work in pairs. Imagine you're organising a party. Make a list of important things to do.

2 Read the article. Does it mention the things on your list?

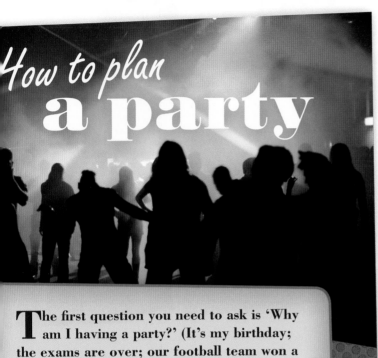

How to plan a party

The first question you need to ask is 'Why am I having a party?' (It's my birthday; the exams are over; our football team won a match; I just want a party.)

All the best parties have a theme. What are you going to choose for yours? Beach party? 1970s disco? Something else? You also need to find ¹_____ to hold your party. Wherever you decide to have it, it's probably a good idea to ²_____ permission from your parents first.

Next, who are you going to invite: ³_____ you know or just some of your friends? It's time to ⁴_____ the guest list. Remember: think carefully about how many people you can afford to invite. When your list is ready, you can ⁵_____ the invitations. Two weeks before the party is the ideal time. Any sooner, and people might forget about the party; any later, and some of your guests might already have other plans.

OK, so now you've got a fortnight to get it all ready. Don't panic – it's plenty of time, but don't leave ⁶_____ until the last minute. If you want to ⁷_____ a DJ, start looking now. Remember that he or she might want you to ⁸_____ a deposit, so make sure you have the money for that. Then you need to ⁹_____ the food and ¹⁰_____ the room, although these things can be left until the day before.

Finally, get a good night's sleep the night before, give yourself a few hours to get the last few things ready and then, most importantly of all, have fun!

3 Read the article again and complete it with the missing words.

get | send out | organise | pay
everyone | hire | decorate
somewhere | draw up | everything

Indefinite pronouns

1 🔊 1.05 Complete the conversation with suitable indefinite pronouns (*everyone*, *somewhere*, *nothing*, etc.). Then listen and check.

TOM Have you got ¹_____ ready for the party?

JADE No, ²_____ is ready. We haven't found ³_____ to have it, for a start. We've looked ⁴_____ .

TOM Have you invited ⁵_____ yet?

JADE Yes, we've invited 50 people and ⁶_____ is coming!

TOM So you've got 50 people coming, but ⁷_____ for them to come to?

JADE That's right.

TOM Well, we've got to do ⁸_____ . How about using my house?

JADE What about your parents?

TOM They won't mind. They're going ⁹_____ for the weekend. I'll make sure ¹⁰_____ is clean and tidy when they get home.

2 Read the next part of the story and continue the conversation. Write four more lines. Use at least one indefinite pronoun.

It's the day after the party. Tom's mum and dad arrive home and open the door…

MUM What's happened? Look at our house!

DAD Tom! TOM!

TOM Oh, hi, Mum. Hi, Dad. You're home early. Did you have a good time?

Arranging a party

SPEAKING Work in pairs to organise a party. Be creative! Think about:

- what it's for
- the theme
- who to invite
- where it will be
- food and drink
- music

C IN MY OPINION, ...
Feeling under the weather

1 **🔊 1.06** Listen to the conversation. What's the matter with Gemma?

2 Complete the conversation with the words.

appointment | should | operation
energy | better | get | physically | took

MUM You don't look well, Gemma. What's up?

GEMMA I'm just tired all the time, Mum. You know, I haven't got any
¹_____ .

MUM Are you sleeping OK?

GEMMA Not great, no. I often wake up in the night.

MUM Well, you know, Gemma, you ²_____ take more exercise. That would help.

GEMMA Really?

MUM Yes. I mean, if you ³_____ more exercise, you'd be more tired ⁴_____ and then you'd sleep better.

GEMMA You're joking, right? I run, I go swimming, I go for long walks. My problem isn't exercise.

MUM Yes, you're right, of course. Well, perhaps you'd ⁵_____ see a doctor. I can ring and make an ⁶_____ for you if you like.

GEMMA A doctor? I don't think so. I don't feel sick – just tired. I'm sure I'll ⁷_____ better soon.

MUM OK, well, we can talk about it later. I'm going out to see a friend of mine who had an ⁸_____ last week.

GEMMA OK, Mum. Hope your friend's all right. And don't worry about me. I'll be fine.

3 Match the verbs 1–6 with a–f to make phrases. Sometimes there's more than one possible combination.

1	feel	a	an appointment
2	get	b	an operation
3	have	c	exercise
4	make	d	a doctor
5	see	e	better
6	take	f	sick

4 Write down as many words related to health as you can think of. Then compare with a partner.

sick
nurse
hospital
...

Giving advice

1 Complete the sentences with *better*, *should* or *ought*.

1 It's late – you'd _____ go.

2 If you aren't well, you _____ to see a doctor.

3 Jane's in hospital. We _____ go and visit her.

4 The doctor is very busy, so you _____ make an appointment. Don't just turn up.

5 Your knee hurts? Well, you'd _____ not play football today, then.

6 If you want to get better, you _____ to rest as much as possible.

2 Match the problems 1–3 with the pieces of advice a–c. Then write one more piece of advice for each problem. Use *had better*, *should* and *ought to*.

1 My hand really hurts. ☐

2 I think I'm going to be late for school. ☐

3 I can't do this homework. ☐

a You'd better hurry.

b Perhaps you should phone a friend.

c You ought to see a doctor.

3 **SPEAKING** Work in pairs. Write mini-dialogues including the problems and advice in Exercise 2. Add two or three lines to each. Then act them out.

Why all these awards?

I'm really tired of awards ceremonies and prizes. Why do we have to compare things? Everywhere you look, there's something going on about who or what is 'the best' or 'the most comfortable' or 'the biggest', and so on. And sometimes the prize winners aren't the best anyway!

Here's an example: the Oscars in 2014. I saw the film *Gravity* and it was the most exciting film I'd ever seen. But did it win the Oscar for Best Film? No! They gave the award to *Twelve Years A Slave*! Can you believe it? It wasn't as good as *Gravity* at all.

OK, *Gravity* was the most successful film at the Oscars – it got seven awards – but I don't think that's enough. Sandra Bullock was fantastic as Dr Ryan. I think she's much better than Cate Blanchett, who won Best Actress. But the good thing is that *Gravity* won Best Visual Effects – I've never seen anything as fantastic. And was the music good? It was great! No other film had music as brilliant as that.

I said all these things to my friend Dave the day after the Oscars. I told him I thought the judges were the craziest people in the world. Dave asked me how many films I'd seen in 2013. I said, 'One – *Gravity*.' Dave says he doesn't know anyone as stupid as me.

Better or worse?

1 Read the blog entry. Mark the sentences T (true) or F (false).

1 The writer likes awards ceremonies. ☐
2 *Gravity* won Best Film at the 2014 Oscars. ☐
3 The writer thinks the visual effects in *Gravity* are the best he's ever seen. ☐
4 Dave thinks the writer is very intelligent. ☐

2 SPEAKING Work in pairs. Discuss these questions.

1 What other awards ceremonies do you know of?
2 Do you like awards ceremonies? Why (not)?
3 Do you think it's fair to compare different movies, actors, music, etc. and choose one as the best?

Comparisons

1 Complete the sentences with the correct form of the adjectives and adverbs. Add any other necessary words.

1 The weather tomorrow won't be _____ (cold) as today.
2 This is the _____ (good) pizza I've ever eaten.
3 Do you think this is _____ (difficult) than the other test?
4 This book's OK, but it isn't the _____ (interesting) one I've ever read.
5 She learns things _____ (easy) than I do.
6 I'm not very good at tennis, but I'm _____ (bad) as Janice!
7 Hurry up! Can't you walk _____ (quick) than that?
8 Do you speak as _____ (loud) your sister?

2 SPEAKING Work in pairs or small groups. Discuss these statements. Do you agree or disagree with them? Why?

1 The best things in life are free.
2 If something is more expensive, it's always better.
3 It's more important to work hard than to play hard.
4 Exercise isn't as important as good sleep.

3 Choose two things or people from one of these categories. Write a paragraph comparing them.

sports that you like | actors that you like
towns or cities that you know | school subjects
books that you have read

D HELP!

Reported speech

1 **Read the story and answer the questions.**

1 What had happened to the caller's computer screen?

2 What three things did Graham ask the caller to do?

3 Why couldn't the caller switch on the lights?

4 What did Graham finally say to the caller?

5 What happened to Graham in the end?

We asked readers to tell us about a time when they tried to help someone. Here's one from Graham Smith.

I used to work in IT for a big company, but I was fired because I got angry with a manager. Here's what happened.

I answered the phone one day and said, 'Hi. Can I help you?' A voice said, 'Hi. I'm a manager in the Sales Department and I've got an IT problem. I need your help.' 'What's the problem?' I asked, and he told me his computer screen had suddenly gone black.

¹_____ , I couldn't think why it had happened. I asked him to check that the screen was still connected. He said it was. ²_____ I asked him if he'd pressed any buttons by mistake. He said, 'No, the computer was installing a program when, suddenly, it went "pooff".'

³_____ a few seconds, I said, 'OK, please check that your computer is still plugged in at the wall. Sometimes it gets disconnected accidentally.' The manager asked me to wait a bit. Then he came back and said, 'I can't see behind my desk where the plug is. It's very dark.' So I told him to switch the light on. Do you know what he said? 'Oh, I can't put the light on because the electricity went off five minutes ago.'

I tried to keep quiet. ⁴_____ , I had to say something. I warned him never to phone me again, ever. He complained to my boss and I was fired. How fair is that, do you think?

2 **Rewrite the sentences in reported speech.**

0 'I need your help.'
He said that _____*he needed my help.*_____

1 'What's the problem?'
I asked him _____

2 'I can't see here because it's very dark.'
He said that _____

3 'Please check that your computer is still plugged in.'
I asked him to _____

4 'I can't put the light on because the electricity went off five minutes ago.'
He said that _____

Sequencing words

Match these words with spaces 1–4 in the story.

a After ☐   c Finally ☐

b Then ☐   d At first ☐

Asking for and offering help

1 **Put the words in order to make questions.**

1 I / you / Can / help / ? ☐

2 help / something / you / me / Could / with / ? ☐

3 me / you / Can / a / lend / hand / ? ☐

4 you / Do / help / any / need / ? ☐

5 you / minutes / got / a / Have / few / ? ☐

2 **Look at the sentences in Exercise 1 again. Mark them A (asking for help) or O (offering help).**

3 **SPEAKING** Work in pairs. Choose a situation and write a conversation in which A asks B for help. Use expressions from Exercise 1. Then act it out.

- A has a problem with some homework.
- A isn't feeling well.
- A's computer isn't working.
- A wants to have a party, but doesn't know where to hold it.

IT problems

1 SPEAKING Work in pairs. What do the pictures show?

A

B

C

2 🔊 1.07 Listen to three conversations. Match them with the pictures in Exercise 1.

3 🔊 1.07 Listen again. In which conversation do you hear these words? Write the number.

a attachment ☐   e install ☐
b coverage ☐   f online ☐
c downloaded ☐ g program ☐
d file ☐   h upload ☐

IT vocabulary

1 Circle the correct words.

1 *go / have* online
2 *post / file* a message
3 *install / key in* your password
4 *install / go* a program
5 *attach / activate* a file
6 *download / go* a file
7 *upload / key* a photo
8 *key / delete* a message
9 *open / install* an attachment
10 *post / buy* an app
11 *upload / activate* flight mode
12 *have / go* network coverage

2 Match the verbs with the nouns. Make as many combinations as you can.

a message | a photo | flight mode | a password
an attachment | a program | a file | an app

0 install   *install a program / an app*
1 attach   _____
2 download   _____
3 upload   _____
4 open   _____
5 post   _____
6 delete   _____
7 activate   _____
8 key in   _____

Passive tenses

1 Complete the sentences from the conversations with the verb forms.

is being repaired | was taken | is installed

1 The photo _____ on a safari trip.
2 Just click on it and the program _____ automatically.
3 The network _____ out here.

2 Rewrite the sentences in the passive.

0 Someone posted a message.
  A message was posted.
1 Someone is downloading a program.
  _____
2 Someone has installed a new program.
  _____
3 Someone has keyed in the password.
  _____
4 Someone is repairing the anti-virus software.
  _____
5 Someone deleted the message.
  _____

3 Describe one of these processes using the passive.
- downloading an app to your mobile phone
- uploading a photo to a social networking site
- installing a program on your computer

1 | LIFE PLANS

READING

1 What are the people doing in the photos? Do you think these are good or bad habits? Why?

2 Tick (✓) the bad habits that you have. Then add two more of your own.

- [ ] not doing enough exercise
- [ ] leaving your homework until the last minute
- [ ] forgetting important dates
- [ ] texting when you shouldn't
- [ ] playing computer games when you should be studying
- [ ] getting up late for school

3 **SPEAKING** Work in pairs. What can you do to change some of these habits?

4 Read the article quickly. What two things is the writer trying to change about her life?

5 **◀))1.08** Read the article again and listen. Mark the sentences T (true) or F (false).

1 The writer has to finish the article by the following day. ☐

2 The writer is finding it easy to lead a healthier life. ☐

3 We use different parts of our brain depending on who we're thinking about. ☐

4 Our brains don't always let us make good choices for our future selves. ☐

5 It takes just under two months for our brains to feel happy with changes to our lifestyles. ☐

6 The writer has decided that she'll never be able to change her habits. ☐

I miss my bad habits

I don't believe it! It's 11 pm and I'm still sitting here writing this article for the school magazine! I've had two weeks to write it and my teacher wants it tomorrow. She's always complaining that I leave things to the last minute. Maybe she's right. A month ago, I made a resolution to be more efficient this year and to never leave things to the last minute. Well, I've failed. At the moment, I guess kids all over the country are thinking back to the resolutions they made at the beginning of the school year. Some of them have already given up for this year. Others are still doing well. Many, I suspect, like me, are struggling with them. I've also been trying to get fitter for four weeks now. I've started going to the gym, I've taken up karate lessons and I've changed my diet. I've even been going to bed earlier. But I'm not feeling any fitter, just a little unhappier. I miss my bad habits. Why is leading a better life so hard?

I've just read an article on a website and I've discovered that it isn't my fault! In fact, it isn't anyone's fault. It's our brains. They're programmed to make it difficult to break bad habits. There's nothing we can do. For example, you're sitting up late playing Minecraft. You know you've got an important test tomorrow, so why don't you just turn off the computer and go to bed? As I said, it's your brain's fault. Scientists have done experiments that show we use one part of our brain when we think about ourselves and another when we think about other people. However, when we think about ourselves in the future, we use the same part of the brain that we usually use to think about other people. In other words, the brain sees the 'future you' as a different person to your 'present you'. And that's why we don't always find it easy to make sensible decisions for ourselves in the future.

But that's not all. Scientists have also discovered that it takes around ten weeks to form a good habit. For example, it's going to take another six weeks before going to the gym stops being so difficult and becomes an automatic part of my life. That's because ten weeks is the amount of time the brain needs to change and accept new behavioural patterns as part of everyday life. The good news is that once you make it to ten weeks, everything becomes a lot easier. The bad news is that ten weeks is a really long time, so it's easy to give up on your good intentions sooner.

So there you are. Maybe we want to change our ways and become better people but our brains won't let us. Or is this just an excuse? Look – I've finished my article on time! Anything is possible!

▮ TRAIN TO THiNK ▮

Reading between the lines

Sometimes a writer doesn't tell us everything directly: we need to draw conclusions from the information the writer gives. We call this 'reading between the lines'.

6 **Answer the questions and give reasons for your answers.**

  0 Who is the writer? (paragraph 1)
    She's a schoolgirl — she's writing for the school magazine and mentions her teacher.
  1 Does the writer feel guilty that she hasn't finished the article? (paragraph 1)
  2 Does she enjoy exercise? (paragraph 1)

SPEAKING

Work in pairs. Discuss these questions.

1 What resolutions are you going to make for this school year?
2 What do you think is the secret of changing your life for the better?

> *Careful planning.*   *Do work first, play later.*

> *Listen to your parents.*

GRAMMAR
Present tenses (review)

1 **Match sentences 1–5 with the tenses a–d and then complete the rule with the names of the tenses.**

1 I'm still **sitting** here writing this article.
2 I've also **been trying** to get fitter for four weeks now.
3 I've **started** going to the gym.
4 I'm **not feeling** any fitter, just a little unhappier.
5 The brain **sees** the 'future you' as a different person to your 'present you'.

a present perfect continuous
b present simple
c present continuous (x2)
d present perfect

RULE:

1 We use the _____ to talk about facts and give opinions.
2 We use the _____ to talk about what's happening at or around the time of speaking.
3 We use the _____ to talk about past actions without saying when they happened.
4 We use the _____ to talk about actions that started in the past and are still happening.

LOOK! We can use the present continuous with *always* to complain about behaviour that we don't like and find annoying.
My dad's always telling me what to do.

2 **Complete the text with the correct present tense forms of the verbs. Sometimes more than one tense is possible.**

It's 2 am and I ¹_____ (lie) in bed. I ²_____ (try) to get to sleep, but I can't. I ³_____ (have) trouble sleeping for about a month now. I ⁴_____ (try) different things to help me sleep, but nothing ⁵_____ (work). My mind ⁶_____ (not want) to stop. A lot ⁷_____ (happen) in my life right now. It's exam time, so I ⁸_____ (study) a lot. There's also the question of next year. I ⁹_____ (think) about it for ages. Mum and Dad ¹⁰_____ (want) me to go to university, but I'm just not sure what to do.

3 **SPEAKING** Work in pairs. Think about a problem you've been having and tell your partner.

I've been fighting a lot with my little brother recently. I've tried to ignore him, but it's impossible.

Workbook page 10

VOCABULARY
Making changes

1 **Match the phrases with the definitions.**

0	make a resolution	*f*
1	give something up	
2	do well	
3	struggle with something	
4	take something up	
5	break a bad habit	
6	form a good habit	
7	change your ways	

a stop doing something
b find something difficult
c start a new hobby or interest
d stop doing something that isn't good for you
e start doing something that is good for you
f decide to make a positive change
g do things differently (usually for the better)
h be successful

2 **Complete the text with the missing verbs.**

Last year I ¹_____ loads of resolutions and decided to ²_____ my ways. I tried to ³_____ the habit of getting up late at weekends. For two months I got up at 8 am. But by 2 pm I felt sleepy, so I ⁴_____ up sleeping in the afternoon. I also ⁵_____ up wasting time online, but my parents bought me a laptop and that was the end of that. Then I stopped eating meat. I was ⁶_____ well until Mum made roast beef. I just had to eat it. I tried to ⁷_____ good habits as well: for example, I started piano lessons. But I ⁸_____ with finding time to practise, so I stopped. This year I've only made one resolution: not to make any resolutions.

3 **SPEAKING** Work in pairs. Discuss these questions.

1 What subjects are you doing well in at school?
2 What subjects do you struggle with?
3 What was the last thing you gave up doing? Why?

Workbook page 12

LISTENING

J.K. Rowling

Sylvester Stallone

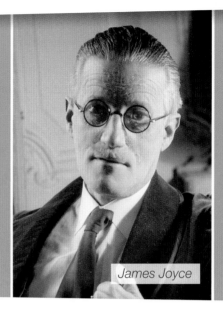

James Joyce

1 **SPEAKING** Work in pairs. Discuss these questions.

  1 What do you know about these people?
  2 Can you match the information with each person?
    A _____ was a famous Irish writer.
    B _____ wrote *Rocky*.
    C _____ wrote the Harry Potter series.

2 ◀))1.09 Listen and check.

3 ◀))1.09 Read the questions carefully. Listen again and make notes.

  1 What's Annie's problem?
  2 What does Ben want to do with his life?
  3 How was James Joyce earning a living when he was 30?
  4 How are the examples of Joyce, Stallone and Rowling different to Annie's situation?
  5 Why does Ben tell Annie not to worry?

4 **SPEAKING** Work in pairs. Compare your answers to Exercise 3.

GRAMMAR
Future tenses (review)

1 Look at the sentences from the listening. Complete them with the correct future forms of the verbs. Then complete the rule with *present continuous*, *going to* and *will*.

  1 I _____ (meet) the careers advisor this afternoon.
  2 I _____ (study) medicine at university.
  3 I'm sure you _____ (do) well whatever you do.

  RULE:
  ● To talk about future arrangements, we often use the [1]_____ .
  ● To make predictions, we often use [2]_____ .
  ● To talk about intentions, we often use [3]_____ .

2 (Circle) the best tense.

  1 *We'll go / We're going* to the beach this Friday. Do you want to come?
  2 I don't think *I'll finish / I'm finishing* this homework.
  3 *I won't go / I'm not going* to university this year. I want to take a year off.
  4 I've got an appointment with the dentist tomorrow. *I'm seeing / I'll see* her at 10 am.
  5 Daisy's learning to fly. *She'll be / She's going to be* a pilot.
  6 I'm not *eating / going to eat* chocolate. That's my resolution for next year.
  7 Argentina *will win / are winning* the next World Cup. That's what I think.
  8 *We're flying / We will fly* on Friday. I'm so excited.

3 Write down:

  1 two arrangements you've got for this week.
  2 two intentions you've got for this year.
  3 two predictions for your life.

Workbook page 11

READING

1 SPEAKING Tick (✓) the statements you agree with. Then discuss them in pairs.

A good friend …

- [ ] always tells you what they're thinking.
- [ ] never criticises you.
- [ ] agrees with everything you say.
- [ ] always listens when you have a problem.

2 Read the article and match the titles with the paragraphs.

- [ ] No one is happy all the time
- [ ] Stop expecting everybody to like you
- [ ] Don't expect people always to agree with you
- [ ] Stop expecting people to know what you're thinking
- [ ] Don't expect people to change

3 Read the article again. Which paragraphs should these people read and think about? There may be more than one possible answer.

1 'Billy's so unfriendly to me. I don't know what I've done wrong.'

2 'Can't they see I don't really feel like talking? I just want them to leave me alone.'

3 'Katie's always got a smile on her face. I wish my life was as perfect as hers.'

4 'I think Jenny would be a brilliant drummer for our band. I don't know what your problem is.'

5 'I wish Dylan wasn't so untidy. He always makes such a mess.'

4 SPEAKING Work in pairs. Discuss these questions.

1 Which piece of advice do you think is the best? Why?

2 What other advice would you add?

For a better life ...

Life can be hard, and when our plans don't work out, it's often easy to blame others. Sometimes we expect too much from friends and family, and when they don't act as we think they should, we feel disappointed. Maybe it would be easier if we stopped expecting so much from other people. No one is perfect, and that includes you.

1 _____

So you want to travel the world before you do a degree, but your parents don't think it's a good idea. Of course, it's great if other people can support you in your decisions, but you can't keep everyone happy all of the time. It's your life and you need to make the decisions to make you happy.

2 _____

Don't worry if there are people who aren't very nice to you, because there are plenty of people who are. They're called your friends. Spend time with them and avoid the others. And when it comes to finding that special person and settling down, remember: there's somebody for everyone.

3 _____

You've been practising football all summer. You think you're good enough to be in the school team, but the teacher doesn't seem to be thinking the same thing. Maybe he just hasn't thought about it at all. He isn't a mind reader, so tell him. Then at least he knows what you're thinking. He might even choose you.

4 _____

People can change, but they don't usually do it because someone else wants them to. You can try and tell them what you're not so happy about, so at least they know, but don't be too disappointed if they carry on doing exactly the same things. You have a choice: accept them or walk away.

5 _____

From their Facebook updates, you'd believe that all your friends are happy all the time and leading exciting lives. Of course, they aren't, just like you know that your life isn't always perfect. We all go through hard times and we often try to hide it. Be kind to people. They might be having a bad day and your smile could make a big difference.

VOCABULARY
Life plans

1 Match the phrases with the pictures.
Write 1–8 in the boxes.

1	retire	5	start a family
2	travel the world	6	settle down
3	start a career	7	get promoted
4	get a degree	8	leave school

A B C D E F G H

2 Complete the text with phrases from Exercise 1.
Use the correct forms of the verbs.

My uncle has always done things differently. He
¹_____ when he was 16 because he wanted to see
other places. He spent the next twenty years
²_____ , working in restaurants and hotels in many
different countries. When he was in his early forties, he
decided to return to the UK. He went to university and
³_____ . He did really well, and when he finished, he
⁴_____ as a translator. Because he was good at his
job, he ⁵_____ quite quickly and he was soon Head
Translator. When he was 48, he met the love of his life
and they decided to ⁶_____ and ⁷_____ .
Now he's 55, with three young children. He says he wants
⁸_____ soon. He wants to stop working and take
the whole family around the world with him. I wouldn't be
surprised if he does.

Workbook page 12

▮ THiNK SELF-ESTEEM ▮

Life changes

1 Complete the table with your own ideas.

	One positive change	One negative change
You leave home	*Freedom*	*You have to look after yourself.*
You do a degree		
You start a career		
You start a family		
You get promoted		
You retire		

2 SPEAKING Work in small groups. Compare your ideas.

WRITING
An email about resolutions

Write an email to an English-speaking friend in another country. Describe your resolutions for the
coming school year. Write about:

- bad habits you're changing • new classes you're taking • activities you plan to take up • why you're doing all of this

What's up with Mia?

1 Look at the photos and answer the questions.

What do you think the problem is?
What does Mia want to give up?

2 🔊 **1.10** Now read and listen to the photostory. Check your answers.

FLORA Hi, Leo. Hi, Jeff.
LEO Hi, Flora.
FLORA Hey, has either of you seen Mia lately?
JEFF No. I haven't seen her for ages, actually.
LEO Now you mention it, neither have I.
FLORA It's strange, isn't it? She hasn't been to the café for a long time. I wonder what she's up to.
LEO Hey, look who it is. Hi, Mia! We were just talking about you. Where have you been hiding?

1

2

MIA Don't even joke about it. I never have time to do anything any more.
FLORA Come and sit down. I'll get you something to drink.
MIA You're a star. That's just what I need.
JEFF So what's up, Mia? Why are you so busy?
MIA Where shall I start? Mondays, I have extra French lessons. Tuesdays, it's tennis lessons. Wednesdays, violin lessons. Thursdays, it's orchestra. Then every night I'm up late doing my homework.
LEO It's Thursday today.
MIA I know. I'm only here because orchestra was cancelled this week. Thank goodness.
LEO Don't you like playing the violin?
MIA Not really. I mean, I like playing an instrument. I just don't think I want to continue with the violin. Do you know I spend up to an hour every day practising?
FLORA So why do you do it?
MIA To keep my mum happy, I suppose.
JEFF You should talk to her, tell her you want to give it up.
MIA Yeah, maybe. But it's not always so easy to talk to her.
FLORA Well, you need to do something. You don't have any time for yourself. I mean, we never get to see you any more.
MIA Yeah, I guess you're right. It's up to me to do something about it.

THE FOLLOWING WEEK ...

3

CHLOE Hi, Mia.
MIA Hi, Chloë.
CHLOE What's up with you? You don't sound very happy.
MIA It's nothing.
CHLOE Really?
MIA Well, to be honest, I don't really feel like orchestra today.
CHLOE Why not?
MIA I haven't had any time to practise. And I'm tired. I don't know if I'm up to it.
CHLOE Don't be silly. I'm sure it'll be fine. Look, Mr Wales wants to start. Come on, Mia.
MIA Here we go. I am *not* looking forward to this.

DEVELOPING SPEAKING

3 Work in pairs. Discuss what you think Mia decides to do. Write down your ideas.

We think that Mia decides to carry on with the violin and continues playing in the orchestra.

4 ▶ EP1 Watch and find out how the story continues.

5 Answer the questions.

1 What happens at orchestra practice?
2 What reasons does Mia give to her mum for giving up the violin?
3 Why does Mia think her mum changed her mind?
4 How is Mia learning the guitar?
5 Why does Mia enjoy playing the guitar?

PHRASES FOR FLUENCY

1 Find these expressions in the photostory. Who says them? How do you say them in your language?

1 Now you mention it, …
2 Where have you been hiding?
3 You're a star.
4 Where shall I start?
5 Don't be silly.
6 Here we go.

2 Use the expressions in Exercise 1 to complete the conversations.

1 A You look tired. Has it been a busy day?
   B Busy? _____ First, I had a Maths test. Then I had Drama club at lunchtime. Then it was a five-kilometre run in PE …
   A Well, you just sit down and I'll get you something to eat.
   B Thanks, Mum. _____

2 A _____, Annie? I haven't seen you for days.
   B I haven't been anywhere. You're the one who disappeared.
   A _____, I have been quite busy.

3 A It's ten o'clock. Time for the test.
   B _____ I'm really not ready for this.
   A Me neither. I've got a feeling I'm not going to pass.
   B _____ You always pass.

WordWise
Phrases with *up*

1 Match the phrases in bold with the definitions.

1 So **what's up**, Mia?
2 Do you know I spend **up to** an hour every day practising?
3 I wonder what she's **up to**.
4 Then every night I'm **up** late doing my homework.
5 It's **up to me** to do something about it.
6 I don't know if I'm **up to** it.

a not in bed
b doing
c what's the matter?
d capable of
e as long as / to a maximum of
f my responsibility

2 Use words and phrases from Exercise 1 to complete the sentences.

1 What have you been _____ recently?
2 I was _____ late watching TV last night.
3 Oh, no! You look really unhappy. _____?
4 It isn't my decision. It's _____ you to decide.
5 He's 75 now, so he isn't _____ long walks.
6 This car can carry _____ six people.

Workbook page 12

Pronunciation
Linking words with *up*
Go to page 120. 🔊

FUNCTIONS
Complaining

1 Match the parts of the sentences.

1 I'm not happy with
2 The problem is that
3 He's always
4 If I'm honest, I don't

a it takes up so much time.
b picking on me.
c really like the violin.
d the way he talks to me.

2 ROLE PLAY Work in pairs. Student A: turn to page 127. Student B: turn to page 128.

2 HARD TIMES

OBJECTIVES

FUNCTIONS: talking about the past
GRAMMAR: narrative tenses (review);
would and *used to*
VOCABULARY: descriptive verbs;
time periods

READING

1 **Look at the pictures and answer the questions.**

1 What do the pictures illustrate?
2 How was life in the past harder than it is today?

2 **Read the article quickly. Make notes on these questions about the Great Fire of London.**

1	In what year did it happen?
2	How did it start?
3	How long did it last?
4	How did people get away?
5	How was the fire stopped?
6	What damage did it do?

3 **Read the article again and listen. Add details to your notes from Exercise 2.**

▌TRAIN TO THiNK ▌

Following an idea through a paragraph

It can be difficult to follow what a writer is trying to say in a longer paragraph. We need to read carefully to understand fully what the writer is saying.

4 **Answer the questions.**

The end of Paragraph 2 says: 'The situation provided the perfect conditions for flames to spread quickly.'

1 Look back at the paragraph. How many things are needed to start a big fire? List them.
2 What were those things in London in 1666?

The beginning of Paragraph 3 says: 'The fire spread quickly but it was also extremely difficult to fight.'

3 Look back at the paragraph. Why was the fire difficult to fight?

The Great Fire of London
The event that changed the face of 17th-century London forever

It was 1 am on Sunday 2 September, 1666. London was sleeping. In a small bakery in Pudding Lane, Thomas Farriner and his workers were busily making bread for the coming day when, suddenly, a fire broke out. Just four days later, thousands of houses had been destroyed and countless people were homeless. How did this happen, and why was the damage so extensive?

For a fire to start, three things are needed: a spark, fuel and oxygen. In the bakery in Pudding Lane, a maid didn't tend to the ovens properly. They got too hot and sparks began to fly. The weather that year had been extremely hot. It hadn't rained for months. But people knew winter was coming, so they'd stocked their cupboards with food and oil. Warehouses were full of wood, coal and other winter supplies. A strong wind was blowing from the east. The situation provided the perfect conditions for flames to spread quickly. What followed was one of the biggest disasters of the 17th-century world.

The fire spread quickly, but it was also extremely difficult to fight. It started in a poor area of the city, where houses were built very close to one another. Tens of thousands of people were living in very small spaces. A simple house was often home to many families as well as lodgers. As the catastrophe struck, people panicked. Some had to smash their doors to get out of their homes. The streets were blocked with people and with material that had fallen from houses. Many people had grabbed their most important possessions and were trying to flee from the flames with them. They screamed in terror and suffered from the heat and the smoke. Some escaped from the city on boats. Others simply dived into the river to save themselves.

The fire had been raging for almost four days when the Duke of York put a plan into action. His soldiers demolished a large warehouse full of paper. This robbed the fire of more fuel and created a 'fire break' that the flames could not jump over. At about this time, the wind also changed direction, driving the fire back into itself. At last, the flames died down enough to be controlled. The fire was finished.

Although surprisingly few people lost their lives, at least 13,000 houses – 80 per cent of the city's buildings – had been destroyed. Thousands of people had become homeless and had lost everything they owned. Gradually, houses were rebuilt in the ruins, but this took several years. Many Londoners moved away from their city and never returned.

SPEAKING

Work in pairs. Discuss these questions.

1 What other events would you suggest for the *Events that shook the world* series? Why?
2 If you had to leave your home in a hurry and had the time to save three things, what would you choose?

GRAMMAR
Narrative tenses (review)

1 **Match the sentences from the article on page 21 with the tenses. Then complete the rule.**

1 London **was sleeping**.
2 Thomas Farriner and his workers **were** busily **making** bread […] when, suddenly, a fire broke out.
3 It **hadn't rained** for months.
4 The fire **had been raging** for almost four days.
5 His soldiers **demolished** a large warehouse.

a past perfect
b past simple
c past continuous (two sentences)
d past perfect continuous

> **RULE:**
> **We use …**
> 1 _____ to talk about finished actions in the past.
> 2 _____ to talk about longer actions in the past interrupted by shorter actions.
> 3 _____ to set the scene.
> 4 _____ to talk about actions before a certain time in the past.
> 5 _____ to talk about uninterrupted actions before a certain time in the past.

2 **Complete the sentences with the past simple or past continuous form of the verbs.**

0 While people _were running_ towards the river, a warehouse _exploded_ . (run / explode)
1 When they _____ how serious the situation was, they _____ their possessions and _____ to get away. (notice / take / try)
2 A man _____ for his family when he _____ a baby in the street. (look / find)
3 While they _____ how to stop the fire, it _____ clear that little could be done. (think / become)
4 While the people in the bakery _____ bread, a small fire _____ . (make / start)

3 **Complete the conversation with the correct form of the verbs. Use the tenses from Exercise 1.**

burn | do | see | run | sit | walk | go | open

IAN   I had a real scare yesterday. As I ¹_____ up to our house, I ²_____ smoke coming from the window.
OLI   ³_____ something _____?
IAN   Fortunately not. I ⁴_____ into the house, ⁵_____ the kitchen door and there was my brother. He ⁶_____ on the floor in shock. He ⁷_____ science experiments! One of them ⁸_____ wrong and exploded.

Workbook page 18

VOCABULARY
Descriptive verbs

1 **Certain verbs make narratives sound more dramatic. Find these words in a dictionary and write down:**

1 what they mean.
2 their past simple and past participle forms.

smash | rage | dive | flee | strike demolish | grab | scream

2 **Replace the underlined words with words from Exercise 1. Change the form if necessary.**

0 He picked up a stone and <u>broke</u> the windscreen of the car.   _smashed_
1 The thief stole a motorbike and <u>escaped</u>.   _____
2 The fires had been <u>burning</u> for days, and no one knew how to stop them.   _____
3 When I got there, I heard somebody <u>shouting</u> with fear.   _____
4 They <u>knocked down</u> the houses to make space for new shops.   _____
5 The man <u>took</u> my wallet <u>from me quickly</u> and ran away.   _____
6 The car lost control and <u>hit</u> another vehicle.   _____
7 He took off his clothes and <u>jumped</u> into the water.   _____

Workbook page 20

Pronunciation
Initial consonant clusters with /s/
Go to page 120.

LISTENING

1 Look at the picture. Why do you think the cow was in court? Choose the best option.

- A It was accused of killing a human.
- B It was interrupting a court meeting.
- C A man was accused of hurting the cow.

2 🔊 1.16 Listen to Ryan's talk. Then answer the questions.

1 When were animals taken to court?
2 In which parts of the world did this happen?

3 🔊 1.16 Listen again. For questions 1–5, choose A, B or C.

1 What were the French rats accused of?
- A entering restaurants
- B taking people's food
- C hunting cats

2 According to the man, why didn't the rats accept their order to appear in court?
- A They hadn't received it.
- B They couldn't read it.
- C They'd never accept an invitation from humans.

3 Why did he say the rats would never go to court?
- A No one would understand them.
- B They might not be safe.
- C They couldn't be friends with humans.

4 How did the other people react to the man?
- A They thought he was crazy.
- B They laughed at him.
- C They couldn't argue against him.

5 What happened to the rats?
- A They were hunted and killed.
- B They were found 'not guilty'.
- C They were ordered to leave the village.

■ THiNK VALUES

Animal rights

1 Read the scenarios. Match them with statements 1–6. There are two statements for each scenario.

Scenario A: ☐ / ☐
Work on a huge multi-million-pound shopping centre has been stopped because nests of an extremely rare frog have been found in the area. It is one of only five places where this frog breeds. The property developers are putting pressure on the local government, saying it will be a disaster for the economy if they aren't allowed to finish the job.

Scenario B: ☐ / ☐
An elderly lady lives on her own. She has family, but they all live far away. A relative has suggested buying her a parrot for her 80th birthday. Other family members are against the idea of keeping an animal in a cage.

Scenario C: ☐ / ☐
There is a hotel that's very popular with tourists because it's close to a beautiful forest. The forest is home to a species of large spider. Although it's harmless, people working in the hotel have been given strict orders to kill any spiders that get into the guest rooms.

1 A bird in a cage can be a great companion for a person who lives alone, so it's the right present.

2 Creating places where people can relax is more important than worrying about a few animals.

3 We can't afford to lose any species of animal.

4 Places where endangered animals have their natural habitat belong to the animals, and not to people.

5 Spiders are ugly and disgusting, and many people are scared of them. Of course they should be killed.

6 Birds need to fly, and they need space to be able to do that. Cages should be forbidden.

2 SPEAKING Which of the statements 1–6 do you agree and disagree with? Why? Make notes of your answers. Then compare your ideas in pairs or small groups.

READING

1 Work in pairs. Look at the pictures, the main title and the paragraph titles. What information do you think each paragraph might contain?

2 Read the article and check your answers.

Family life
in 17th-century Britain

By the 17th century, life in Europe had started to become more comfortable for those who had money. Trade had become more important, and the number of people who could read and write was starting to grow. But while the rich were enjoying good food, poetry and the theatre, life for the poor hadn't changed much at all. Here are a few examples of what ordinary family life was like in the olden days.

A typical household

Women used to have seven or eight children, but one in every three children died before reaching one year of age. Many children had

to leave home when they were as young as seven years old to work as shepherds or helpers on farms. There weren't many elderly people in the families because people died much younger than they usually do today. Few people expected to live beyond 40. In fact, children frequently grew up without parents at all.

A crowded life

Ordinary people used to live in one-room houses, together with chickens, goats or even cows. Only richer families had mattresses. On cold nights, everyone in the family would crowd together to sleep, to warm each other up. Unfortunately, this had a bad effect on people's health. Lice infestations were very common, and if one person suffered from an illness, everybody else would get it

too. Taking a bath was such a rare event that everybody smelled bad.

Childcare

Life didn't allow people to spend a lot of time with their children. Parents used to leave even very young children on their own for most of the day. Records from that time report many stories of children who got too close to the fire and burned to death. But even when parents were with their children, they didn't care for them in the ways we're used to parents doing today. Children were often simply considered workers. Parents didn't use to sing songs to their children or play with them. It used to be normal to call a child 'it' rather than 'he' or 'she'.

It's often easy to fantasise about the past and think how wonderfully simple life was compared to all the pressure we face in our day-to-day lives. But was it really so great? For most people, it probably wasn't.

3 Read the article again. Mark the sentences T (true) or F (false). Correct the false sentences.

1 Life in the 17th century was difficult for everybody, no matter how much money they had. ☐

2 Grandparents often used to live with the families and look after the young children. ☐

3 There wasn't a lot of space in most people's homes and they often shared it with their animals. ☐

4 Children sometimes died because their parents weren't very concerned about their safety. ☐

5 Parents these days spend more time with their children than they did in the olden days. ☐

4 **SPEAKING** Work in pairs. Discuss these questions.

1 Compare family life in the 17th century with family life now. What are the most striking differences?

2 What do you think life will be like 100 years from now? Will it be easier? If so, how?

GRAMMAR
would and used to

1 Complete these sentences from the article on page 24. Then complete the rule with *used to / didn't use to* and *would(n't)*.

1 Women _____ have seven or eight children.
2 On cold nights, everyone in the family _____ crowd together to sleep, to warm each other up.
3 Parents _____ sing songs to their children or play with them.
4 It _____ be normal to call a child 'it' rather than 'he' or 'she'.

> **RULE:** To talk about habits and repeated actions in the past, we can use *used to / didn't use to* or *would(n't)*.
> - We use [1]_____ with both action and stative verbs.
> - We only use [2]_____ with action verbs.

2 (Circle) the correct words. Sometimes both options are possible.

1 When I was a child, I *would / used to* play a lot with my sister.
2 We *would / used to* have a cat, Tubby.
3 We *would / used to* like her a lot and play with her all the time.
4 It's funny, but I *would / used to* think I'd never learn to read.
5 We *would / used to* share a bedroom.
6 My sister and I *would / used to* be such good friends!

3 Complete the sentences and conversations with the correct form of *used to*.

1 A _____ you _____ have a pet when you were a child?
  B Yes, I _____ have a cat.
2 We _____ have a car. We used to walk everywhere.
3 A _____ you _____ watch a lot of TV when you were younger?
  B Yes, I _____ watch it every day when I got home from school.
4 I _____ like vegetables, but I love them now.
5 A _____ your dad _____ read you stories before you went to bed?
  B No, he didn't, but my mum _____ .
6 I _____ like having birthday parties. I was a really shy child.

Workbook page 19

VOCABULARY
Time periods

Look at phrases 1–9 and match them with categories a–c. Compare your answers with the class.

a the present
b the recent past
c a long, long time ago in history

	1	from 1995 until 2004
	2	in the Middle Ages
	3	in this day and age
	4	these days
	5	in the olden days
	6	in the last century
	7	not so long ago
	8	a decade ago
	9	nowadays

Workbook page 20

FUNCTIONS
Talking about the past

Work in pairs. Choose a topic for your partner and a period in the past. Your partner makes a comparison between the present and that time period. Take turns.

school | food | technology
games | home | travel

games in the 1930s

Well, children would play with teddy bears or dolls. These days, many children have electronic games.

Culture

1 **Look at the photos and answer the questions.**

1 In what part of the world were these photos taken?

2 Why might life be difficult there? How many reasons can you think of?

2 🔊 1.17 **Read and listen to the article. Check your predictions.**

Where life is really hard

It's the end of the winter. Most people have been inside for weeks. They haven't seen the sun for a long time. But some men are outside. It's bitterly cold, with temperatures of around -45° Celsius, and the freezing wind makes the situation difficult for them to bear. These men are hunters, and the survival of the people they've left behind in the villages depends on how successful their hunt is.

Akycha is one of these men. He's been out hunting for more than a week now. While he's away from home, he stays overnight in a little igloo that he's made himself from ice and snow. The igloo protects him from the freezing wind. Inside, there's a little stove for cooking, and a small stone lamp which provides light. Together, they help to create a temperature of around 12° Celsius.

Right now, Akycha is several kilometres away from his igloo. He's riding his snowmobile along the coast, far out on the frozen sea. Suddenly, he can see something in the distance. He stops his snowmobile and checks through his binoculars. It's a seal. Holding a screen of white canvas in front of him in one hand, and his gun in the other, he moves forward, cautiously hiding behind the screen all the time so that the seal won't notice him. If he's lucky and his hunt goes well, the meat he brings home should last his family for several weeks.

Akycha and his people are part of the Inuit community. Most of them still live a very traditional life, a life that makes them dependent on hunting seals and whales. Some of them also live off the reindeer they keep.

The Inuit are indigenous people of the Arctic Circle, which means they've lived here for so long that they feel the land is theirs. The Arctic Circle is a huge land area that belongs to a number of northern countries: Russia, the USA, Canada, Greenland, Norway, Sweden, Finland and Iceland. The northern environment is an exceptional habitat. Temperatures are low during most of the year and summers are short, which means that plants can only grow for a few weeks every year. If the reindeer eat the moss that grows in a certain area, it can take up to 30 years for the plants to grow back. This is why Inuits who make a living from keeping and breeding reindeer have to be constantly on the move with their herds.

For most of us, life is less hard than it is for the Inuit people. But maybe we can learn something from them. Their traditional way of life is a model of living in partnership with nature, rather than exploiting and destroying it.

3 **Read the article again. Answer the questions.**

1 What are winters like inside the Arctic Circle?

2 How does Akycha survive when he's out hunting?

3 What does he hunt and how does he do this?

4 Why can't the Inuit who keep reindeer stay in one place for a long time?

4 **SPEAKING Work in pairs. Discuss these questions.**

1 In what other areas of the world do people live under extreme conditions?

2 What is the coldest or hottest place you've ever been in? What was the experience like for you?

3 Would you find it easier to live in an area where it's very cold or very hot?

5 VOCABULARY There are eight highlighted words or phrases in the article. Match them with these definitions.

1 continue to be enough
2 not taken with them
3 from one evening, through to the next morning
4 not staying in one place for very long
5 tolerate, put up with
6 large groups of animals
7 a type of plant
8 raising (animals)

WRITING

A magazine article about a historical event

1 Read the article. What happened in Berlin in these years?

1 1961   2 1989   3 1990

2 Find examples in the article of:

1 a sentence containing the past simple and the past continuous.
2 the past perfect.
3 the past perfect continuous.
4 descriptive verbs.
5 expressions referring back to the past.

3 The article has three paragraphs. Which of them:

1 sets the scene for the main events?
2 describes the main action?
3 describes the historical background?

4 Think of an event that shook the world.

- Do some Internet research to find out more about it.
- Choose the most important and interesting details.
- Organise the information into paragraphs.
- Think about the language you'll need to describe the event.

5 Write an article for a school magazine about an event that shook the world (200 words).

The fall of the Berlin Wall

For 28 years, Berlin was a divided city. Ever since its construction in 1961, a huge wall had stopped citizens from East Germany visiting their neighbours in the west. Many people had tried. Some were successful, but many more died, shot as they attempted to get to the other side.

In 1989, there were a number of radical political demonstrations across Eastern Europe, as the people of countries such as Poland and Hungary protested against their governments and managed to change them. On 9 November, the East German government announced that their people were free to visit the western side of the city.

That evening, thousands of East Berliners rushed to the wall and demanded that the gates were opened. The border guards didn't know what to do. While the crowds were singing, the guards phoned their bosses for orders. It soon became clear that they had no choice but to let the people pass. On the other side, the crowds were greeted by West Berliners with flowers and champagne. People climbed up onto the top of the wall and began dancing on it to celebrate their new freedom. People started arriving with sledgehammers to try and smash down the wall. Many grabbed bricks as souvenirs. A little later, the government sent in bulldozers to demolish the wall. The wall that had been dividing a city for nearly three decades was soon gone and, 339 days later, the two nations of East and West Germany also became one.

READING AND USE OF ENGLISH
Part 1: Multiple-choice cloze
Workbook page 17

1 **For questions 1–8, read the text below and decide which answer (A, B, C or D) best fits each gap. There is an example at the beginning (0).**

0   A (stopped)   B finished   C ended   D not

Do you ever stop and think about how easy the Internet has made our lives? I know there are times when it's slow or has **(0)** ___ working altogether, times when maybe you feel like **(1)** ___ your computer screen into tiny pieces. But just think of all those things you use it for. You want to buy the new One Direction CD – you can **(2)** ___ online and buy it. You need to **(3)** ___ some research for your homework – you can find it all there on the web. You feel like a **(4)** ___ with your best friend, so you Skype them. You just want a **(5)** ___ from your homework, so you start up Minecraft or whatever game it is you prefer and start playing. These **(6)** ___ everything we need is just a click of a button away.

Of course, it wasn't always like this. Only a few decades **(7)** ___ , people had to do things like go to the shops if they wanted to buy something and often those shops were closed! They had to look in very large, heavy books called encyclopedias to find information. They had to **(8)** ___ up the telephone if they wanted to talk and if their best friend wasn't at home, they simply couldn't talk to them. That's how tough life was. And these poor people who had to suffer such hardships were … our parents! Makes you feel sorry for them, doesn't it?

1	A	demolishing	B	striking	C	smashing	D grabbing
2	A	come	B	enter	C	click	D go
3	A	do	B	make	C	find	D ask
4	A	talking	B	chat	C	question	D speak
5	A	break	B	stop	C	end	D fix
6	A	times	B	ages	C	years	D days
7	A	after	B	since	C	ago	D past
8	A	take	B	pick	C	grab	D hold

SPEAKING
Part 1: Interview
Workbook page 25

2 **In pairs, ask and answer the questions.**

1 Who do you spend the most time with at the weekends, and what do you do with them?
2 What kind of films do you like best? What do you like about them?
3 Where did you go for your last holiday? What was it like?
4 What's your favourite sport to play? What do you like about it?
5 What things do you enjoy doing the most with your parents?
6 What is your favourite room in your home and why do you like it?
7 If you could be anywhere now, where would it be and why?
8 What things do you like to do at home on a rainy day?
9 Who is your best friend and what do you like the most about him/her?

VOCABULARY

1 Complete the sentences with the words in the list. There are four extra words.

break | change | do | form | give up | grab | make
scream | retire | settle | smash | strike | struggle | travel

1 It would be wonderful to _____ around the world one day.
2 It's a really bad habit – I need to _____ it soon.
3 He would always arrive late, and no one could make him _____ his ways.
4 Good luck with the test – I'm sure you'll _____ really well.
5 Every 31st December, I _____ a resolution to do something, but I usually break it!
6 I saw a man _____ that woman's purse and run away.
7 On her 65th birthday, she decided to _____ and travel the world.
8 I need more time to study for my exams, so I'm going to _____ my judo classes for a while.
9 I think he's going to break the record – in fact, he's going to _____ it!
10 They were so excited by the concert that they started to _____ really loudly. /10

GRAMMAR

2 Complete the sentences with the phrases in the list. There are two extra phrases.

was looking | would look | 'm seeing | are going to | go to | used to love | see | 'll love

1 I _____ my aunt and uncle once a month.
2 Four or five of us _____ eat pizza tonight.
3 Have fun at the concert – I'm sure you _____ it!
4 When I was a kid, I _____ going to the river to swim.
5 I'm not very well, so I _____ the doctor tomorrow.
6 When I saw her, she _____ in a shop window.

3 Find and correct the mistake in each sentence.

1 When he was young, my dad used to reading books about nature.
2 When I got to the house, there was no one there. The party finished!
3 I am running in the park every morning before school.
4 We're really excited because we will go on holiday next week.
5 He was tired because he had been running two kilometres.
6 While I was cycling in the park, I was falling off my bicycle. /12

FUNCTIONAL LANGUAGE

4 Circle the correct words.

1 A I'm angry with Jack. He's *always / often* picking on me.
   B I know. He's horrible. *I don't like / I'm not liking* him at all.
2 A You know, in the *past / olden* days, people didn't have the Internet.
   B I know! But *these days / not so long ago* we can get information so quickly!
3 A Gina and I *have / are having* lunch tomorrow. Why don't you come too?
   B Great – thank you! *I see / I'll see* you at the restaurant! /8
4 A No one *uses / is using* typewriters any more.
   B Not in *nowadays / this day and age*, no!

MY SCORE /30

| 22 – 30 |
| 10 – 21 |
| 0 – 9 |

3 WHAT'S IN A NAME?

OBJECTIVES

FUNCTIONS: giving advice; expressing obligation; giving recommendations, warnings and prohibitions

GRAMMAR: (don't) have to / ought to / should(n't) / must; had better (not); can('t) / must(n't)

VOCABULARY: making and selling; expressions with *name*

READING

1 **Look at the names and logos and answer the questions.**

1 These are the names and logos of various companies. What kind of products do they offer?

> *Jaguar sells cars.*

2 Add two more names of companies or products that are famous around the world.

2 **SPEAKING** **Work in pairs. Some people think the name of a brand is very important. What do you think is the reason for this?**

3 **Read the blog entry quickly. Which of the brands shown above does it mention?**

4 **◀) 1.18** **Read the blog entry again and listen. Answer the questions.**

1 Why do companies think a lot about a brand name?
2 What makes a good brand name?
3 Why were each of these names chosen?
  Jaguar | Pret A Manger | WhatsApp
4 Why was Nova a bad name for a car in Spain?
5 Why do some teenagers choose to buy more expensive products (like clothes)?

▮ TRAIN TO THiNK ▮

Identifying the main topic of a paragraph

Writers use a new paragraph when they want to change the topic. The opening line of a paragraph usually gives you a clue about its topic.

5 **Look at paragraphs 3 and 4. What is the topic of each paragraph? Tick (✓) two options.**

A what teenagers wear to school ☐
B brand names are important in the teenage market ☐
C some really bad brand names ☐
D ways to pick a brand name ☐

Brand names

1 OK, so imagine you've thought of a great idea for a product to make and sell – a game, or an app, or some clothes, for example. You know you can sell millions of them, but first of all, you must give the product a name – a brand name. And that may not be as easy as you think.

2 The brand name is the thing that distinguishes your product from all the others, and it's really important that it makes an impact. Businesses spend a lot of time thinking about brand names; when the name has been picked, it's very difficult to change, so companies have to get it right first time.

3 So how do you choose a name? A brand name ought to be unique, memorable and easy to understand. It should create some kind of emotional connection with people who buy the product – the target market. Some companies use the family name. When Henry Ford started making cars, he just called the company Ford. But you don't have to use a family name – you can go for an image. Staying with cars, think about the brand name Jaguar, a beautiful but dangerous wild cat. What does that say about the manufacturer's product? Some companies use wordplay. It's a common technique for naming apps, for example WhatsApp (from the English expression What's up?). Others like to use foreign words because they sound special or different. For example, in Britain and the USA there's a chain of sandwich shops with the French name Pret A Manger, which means 'ready to eat'. And what do you have to be careful about? Well, you shouldn't choose a name that might not work in certain countries or cultures.

Many years ago, a car company launched a new car that they called Nova. They thought it suggested something nice and new, but in Spanish it can be read as no va ('it doesn't go'). Not a good name for a car in Spain, then!

4 These days, the choice of brand name is particularly important if your product is targeted at the teenage market. Teenage consumers are perhaps more concerned with brand names and company logos than any other group. When a brand, especially a clothing brand, becomes popular with teenagers, then there's a lot of pressure to wear those clothes and have the name and/or logo visible. A teacher in an American high school said: 'I certainly see that kids are obsessed with brand names. They won't buy something that's almost identical – and cheaper – simply because they feel they must wear something with the right logo.' So if you want to get into the teenage market, you have to find a product and a brand name that works with that age group, and create some great advertisements too.

5 Companies know that the name isn't everything – the product itself has to be good, of course – but it's an essential part of the package.

'I'm so glad that we don't have to wear school uniforms any more!'

SPEAKING

Work in pairs. Discuss these questions.

1 Can you think of any more brand names which:
   a use a family name?
   b try to create an image?
   c are in another language?
2 Have you ever bought or wanted something just because of the brand? Give examples.

GRAMMAR

(don't) have to / ought to / should(n't) / must

1 **Complete the sentences from the article on page 31. Then complete the rule with** *have to*, *don't have to*, *ought to*, *should*, *shouldn't* **and** *must*.

1 First of all, you _____ give the product a name.

2 Companies _____ get it right first time.

3 A brand name _____ be unique, memorable and easy to understand.

4 But you _____ use a family name.

5 And what _____ you _____ be careful about?

6 Well, you _____ choose a name that might not work in certain countries or cultures.

> **RULE:** We use ^{1}_____ or _____ to say 'this is important or necessary'. We use ^{2}_____ to say 'this isn't important or necessary'. We use ^{3}_____ or _____ to tell someone that something is a good idea. We use ^{4}_____ to tell someone that something isn't a good idea. (*Ought to* isn't as frequent as *should*. It is used mostly in writing, and the negative form is rare.)

2 **Complete the conversation with the correct form of** *have to*.

MANDY   Mum, there's a new mobile phone out. It's brilliant. I ^{1}_____ get one!

MUM   No way! Your mobile phone is fine. You ^{2}_____ buy another one.

MANDY   But you know what it's like at school. Everyone ^{3}_____ have the latest product!

MUM   Yes, and it's terrible. Why ^{4}_____ you all _____ wear the same clothes, for example?

MANDY   Because it's what teenagers do. You were young once. Don't you remember?

MUM   I see. And I ^{5}_____ go to work to pay for all these things, right?

MANDY   Oh, Mum! You ^{6}_____ be difficult!

3 **Complete the conversation with suitable modal verbs. There is often more than one possible answer.**

GILL   The new café is great – you ^{1}_____ go there.

JACK   I've heard it's a bit expensive.

GILL   Yes, that's true. You ^{2}_____ go there every day. But you ^{3}_____ try the cakes – they're delicious!

JACK   OK. What's the place called, anyway?

GILL   Can you believe it's called The Coffee Shop?!

JACK   What a boring name! You ^{4}_____ be a genius to think of that!

GILL   They ^{5}_____ have a foreign name, like Le Café.

JACK   Well, OK. But it ^{6}_____ be easy to pronounce. There's a shop in town called Arighi Bianchi and no one knows how to say it.

GILL   But the owner is Italian. It's his name!

JACK   I guess I ^{7}_____ know that. Anyway, I ^{8}_____ go home and do my homework for tomorrow.

GILL   You ^{9}_____ worry about that. It's easy.

JACK   Really? OK, so let's go to the cinema. There's a new film that we ^{10}_____ see!

Workbook page 28

VOCABULARY
Making and selling

1 **Complete the sentences with the words.**

advertisement | brand | chain | consumers
image | logo | manufacturer | products

1 They make cleaning _____ , like washing powder.

2 The prices have gone up a lot, so now _____ have to pay more.

3 I always buy the same _____ of shoes – they're so comfortable.

4 It's a _____ that has shops in every town.

5 That shop has a really funny _____ on TV.

6 The Nike _____ is a large tick.

7 When the company's director went to prison it damaged the company's _____ .

8 If it doesn't work, send it back to the _____ .

2 **SPEAKING Answer the questions. Then work in pairs and compare your answers.**

Can you name …

1 three places where you find advertisements?

2 a manufacturer of mobile phones?

3 a chain of shops and a chain of restaurants?

4 one thing you always buy the same brand of?

Workbook page 30

LISTENING

1 🔊 1.19 **Listen to Paul talking to his teacher, Mrs Jenkins. What is their conversation about?** (Circle) **the correct option.**

A how to remember names
B why some names are hard to remember
C why some people can't remember names

2 🔊 1.19 **Listen again. Mark the sentences T (true) or F (false).**

1 Mrs Jenkins has taught Paul's class three times. ☐
2 Paul isn't good at remembering people's names. ☐
3 Mrs Jenkins says you have to concentrate if you want to remember names. ☐
4 Mrs Jenkins thinks it's useful to say the person's name as soon as you hear it. ☐
5 She remembered Paul's name because she knows another person called Paul. ☐
6 She always remembers people's names. ☐

GRAMMAR
had better (not)

1 Complete these sentences from the listening. Then (circle) **the correct words to complete the rule.**

1 I _____ go now.
2 You _____ be late for your next class.

> **RULE:** We use *had ('d) better* to warn someone that bad things will happen if they [1]*do / don't do* something. We use *had ('d) better not* to warn someone that bad things will happen if they [2]*do / don't do* something.

2 Complete the sentences with *had better (not)*.

1 The bus goes in two minutes. You _____ run.
2 I'll lend you my pen – but you _____ break it!
3 It's going to rain. We _____ go inside.
4 You have to get up very early tomorrow, so you _____ go to bed. It's 1 am.
5 You _____ eat any more sweets. You'll be sick.

> Workbook page 29

FUNCTIONS
Giving advice

1 🔊 1.20 **Put the sentences in the correct order to make two conversations. Then listen and check.**

1 ☐ LIAM Why? What's her name?
  ☐ LIAM What's the matter, Jo?
  ☐ LIAM Well, you'd better get some help – quickly!
  ☐ JO It's something like Sharita Wass Ikonor.
  ☐ JO I've got to phone someone and I've no idea how to pronounce her name.

2 ☐ BOB Well, I wrote the wrong name in my birthday card to her son. I called him Jason, not Jacob.
  ☐ BOB I know. She's really cross.
  ☐ BOB My sister's really angry with me.
  ☐ MIA Why?
  ☐ MIA You'd better not do that again!

2 Work in pairs. Imagine you forgot your best friend's birthday. Write a conversation using *had better (not)*.

▉ THiNK SELF-ESTEEM ▉
People and their names

1 Complete the questionnaire (1 = I strongly agree; 5 = I strongly disagree).

1 I find it easy to remember people's names. ☐
2 I only remember the names of people I like. ☐
3 I hate it when people forget my name. ☐
4 Your name is an important part of who you are. ☐
5 I feel sorry for people who have unusual names. ☐

2 SPEAKING **Compare your answers in small groups. Which question(s) do you agree on?**

READING

1 **Look at the names and answer the questions.**

Apple Martin | Brooklyn Beckham | Moon Unit Zappa

1 Do you know anything about these people?

2 Think of one thing that they have in common.

2 **These are eight names that parents tried to call their children. Which do you think were allowed (✓) or not allowed (✗) by the government?**

☐ 1 Talula does the Hula from Hawaii

☐ 2 Fish and Chips

☐ 3 Number 16 Bus Shelter

☐ 4 Google

☐ 5 Ikea

☐ 6 Q

☐ 7 Pluto

☐ 8 Monkey

Brooklyn Beckham

Moon Unit Zappa

3 **Read the article and check your answers to Exercise 2.**

4 **Read the article again. Answer the questions.**

1 Which people's unusual names do we often hear about?

2 What reason did a New Zealand judge give for not allowing some names?

3 What did Mariléia dos Santos decide to do?

4 What did she become well known for?

5 Why did David Carradine give his son an unusual name?

5 SPEAKING **Mark each statement with a number from 1 to 5 (1 = I strongly agree; 5 = I strongly disagree).**

a Parents should be able to give their children any name they want.

b Children with silly names should be allowed to change them when they're 12 years old.

c It doesn't matter what name a child has because they can change it as an adult.

d Every country should have a list of names that parents are allowed to give their children.

6 SPEAKING **Compare your answers with other people in the class.**

Crazy names

Names for your children: it's always a big question for parents. Should you give them an 'ordinary' name or do you want something a bit different? We always hear about big names in the world of cinema, music or sport who prefer something that isn't ordinary. And so they give their kids names like Apple or Brooklyn or Moon Unit. Other people like to use brand names for their children, so there are now quite a few people called Armani or Diesel running around in school playgrounds.

So can you call your child anything you want? Well, it depends where you live. In New Zealand, for example, you can't call your child Talula Does The Hula From Hawaii, and you can't call your twins Fish and Chips. (And yes, parents in New Zealand really have tried to give their kids these names.)

It's hard to believe, but you can call a child Number 16 Bus Shelter. Generally, certain names aren't allowed because, as a New Zealand judge said in one case, 'a name mustn't make a fool of the child'. In Sweden, if you want the name Google for your kid, then go ahead – no problem. But you'd better not try to call your children Ikea or Q, because the government won't let you. Things are even more difficult in Denmark. There's an official list of about 7,000 approved names, and parents need special permission to use a name that isn't on it. Pluto and Monkey didn't get on it.

Of course, when kids grow up, they can decide to change their name, and then it's a different game altogether. If a woman footballer wants to call herself Michael Jackson, which is what Brazilian player Mariléia dos Santos decided to do, then there's nothing to stop her. (She made a name for herself as one of the best female footballers in the world.) And, of course, singers do it all the time. Shawn Corey Carter and Stefani Germanotta, for example, might not be household names today if they hadn't decided to use the stage names Jay-Z and Lady Gaga. Some people, however, change their name from something unusual to something ordinary in order to blend in. David Carradine named his son Free because he wanted him to feel free to do anything, even to change his name – which he did, to Tom.

GRAMMAR
can('t) / must(n't)

1 Complete these sentences from the listening on page 33 and the article on page 34. Then complete the rule with *can*, *can't* and *mustn't*.

1 _____ I ask you something?
2 You _____ call your twins Fish and Chips.
3 You _____ call a child Number 16 Bus Shelter.
4 A name '_____ make a fool of the child'.

> **RULE:** To talk or ask about permission, we often use the modal verb [1]_____ . To say what isn't allowed, we often use [2]_____ or _____ .

2 Complete the sentences with *mustn't* and the verbs. Then match them with the pictures.

run | talk | be | miss

1 You _____ so loudly!
2 I _____ be late.
3 I _____ the goal!
4 You _____ .

3 Rewrite the sentences using modal verbs from this unit and the pronouns in brackets. There is often more than one possible answer.

0 Diving isn't allowed. (you) *You can't dive here.*
1 It isn't necessary for us to wear uniforms. (we)
2 It's a good idea to buy a new phone. (you)
3 It's OK for you to use my laptop. (you)
4 It's necessary for them to work harder. (they)
5 Are we allowed to play here? (we)

Workbook page 29

VOCABULARY
Expressions with *name*

1 Match the underlined expressions with the definitions.

1 Tony Hawk is <u>a big name</u> in skateboarding.
2 He's upset because some of the other kids <u>call him names</u>.
3 Jay-Z isn't his real name – it's his <u>stage name</u>.
4 Fish, meat, vegetables, fruit – <u>you name it</u>, I eat it.
5 Look! It's <u>what's-his-name / what's-her-name</u>.
6 We want to get married, but we haven't <u>named the day</u> yet.
7 I know you don't want to do the exams, but it's <u>the name of the game</u> for university entry.
8 He <u>made a name for himself</u> as a great actor.

a decide the date of an event, often a wedding
b someone whose name I can't remember
c the most important part of something
d a person who is important or famous in their profession
e a name that a person (usually an actor or a singer) uses in their profession
f use rude names about, or to, a person
g become known or respected by many people
h anything you say (or choose)

2 Complete the missing word(s).

1 She's been to Europe, Asia and Australia – you _____ _____ , she's been there!
2 Hard work is the _____ of _____ _____ if you want to do well in your exams.
3 My uncle's a doctor. He's a _____ _____ in the field of cancer research.
4 Some of her classmates _____ her _____ . It's horrible for her.
5 You're engaged? That's wonderful! When are you going to _____ _____ day?
6 Oh look! There's _____-his-_____ – you know, that boy who lives in your street.
7 She made _____ _____ for _____ on a reality TV show and became a famous singer.
8 Bruno Mars is the _____ name of Pete Gene Hernandez.

Workbook page 30

> ### Pronunciation
> Strong and weak forms: /ɒv/ and /əv/
> **Go to page 120.**

Fiction

1 🔊 **1.23** Read and listen to the introduction and the first part of the extract. Answer the questions.

1 What is Tess's full name?
2 In the company, her name is used to mean something. What, and why?

Wild Country by Margaret Johnson

Tess and Grant are tour leaders for a group walking holiday in France. But they don't get on well – at least at the start …

'I didn't ask to work with you,' Grant said, 'and I know you didn't ask to work with me. But here we are, so shall we at least try to get on with each other?' I looked back at him crossly. 'I'll try if you try,' I said, but I didn't like the smile he gave me.

I'd been a tour leader for Wild Country, my father's walking holiday company, for a year. In that time I'd been late meeting a group at the airport several times. I'd also lost my wallet, with all the money to buy food for the tour group for a week in it. And, of course, everybody who worked for Wild Country knew about the time I'd taken a group to the wrong town on the wrong day. They'd all missed their plane home. Now, *that* was a very famous mistake.

My mistakes were so famous in the company that doing something wrong was called 'doing a Tess Marriot'. I think it was Grant Cooper who started saying that, actually – horrible man.

2 🔊 **1.24** Read and listen to the second part of the extract. Mark the sentences T (true) or F (false).

1 Tess thinks her father's idea was a bad one. ☐
2 She's happy when she arrives at the airport. ☐
3 She tries hard to smile when she goes into the airport. ☐
4 She likes Grant because he laughs a lot. ☐
5 She helps Grant to find the group of tourists. ☐

And now my father had arranged for me to work with Grant Cooper on this tour. He thought I would learn something from Grant — something to make me a better tour leader. I thought my father was wrong. I was just too different to Grant; and I didn't *want* to be like him anyway.

After thirty minutes in a hot bus with these thoughts going round and round my head I felt very fed up. Which was the opposite of how I should be when I meet a group at the start of a holiday.

'A tour leader should smile as often as possible.' That's what it said in the book I was given when I started the job. 'At the beginning of a tour, holidaymakers are often tired from their journeys. They may also be worried about what the other people on the holiday will be like. A smile from you makes everybody feel better.'

So as I entered the airport building I tried to put a smile on my face. But it was difficult to keep it there as I tried, without luck, to find my group.

'Wild Country, Walking in Provence?' I asked any group of more than four people, but they all looked at me as if I was mad. I was beginning to think I'd got the wrong time or come to the wrong airport when I saw *him* — Grant Cooper. My heart immediately gave a jump, and not just because I was nervous about being late. I didn't like Grant, but he was very good-looking. I'd liked the look of him when I first met him. But then I'd spoken to him, and all that changed.
I just didn't find him easy to get on with. Every time he spoke to me I felt he was laughing at me. It made me so mad I wanted to scream.

As I got closer, I could see that Grant had already found the group. There was nothing else to do but walk up to them with a big Wild Country smile on my face.

'Hello, everybody,' I said. 'I'm Tess Marriot, one of your tour leaders. I hope you had a good journey?'

'Hello, Tess,' Grant said. 'Did you get lost on your way to the airport?'

3 **SPEAKING** Work in pairs. Discuss these questions.

1 Imagine you're Tess. What's your answer to Grant's question at the end of the extract?

2 In the extract we learn that 'doing a Tess Marriot' means making a mistake.

  a Think of a famous person who is well known for certain actions or qualities. How could that person's name be used?

  > I think 'doing a Beyoncé' could mean singing really well and dancing at the same time.

  b How would you like *your* name to be used?

WRITING
A reply to a letter asking for advice

1 **Read the letter and the reply. Answer the questions.**

  1 What is Alan's problem?
  2 What question does Susannah suggest that Alan asks himself?

2 **Complete the missing words from Susannah's reply.**

  1 This is the first question you _____ _____ ask yourself.
  2 If the answer is no, then maybe _____ _____ end the friendship now.
  3 … you _____ _____ talk to him about the name-calling …
  4 … and explain that he _____ _____ stop saying those things.
  5 Finally, _____ _____ _____ _____ to talk to your parents.

3 **Read Susannah's reply again. In which paragraph does she …**

  1 offer advice to make the friendship work?
  2 outline Alan's problem?
  3 tell him to speak to others about his problem?
  4 ask Alan to think more carefully about the situation?

4 **Read another letter to Susannah. Write three pieces of advice for Lara.**

5 **Write a reply to Lara (150–200 words). Say what you think she should do.**

Susannah's advice page

Write with your problem and Susannah will give you advice. This week's letter is from Alan in Salisbury, UK.

Dear Susannah,

Last month, we moved to a new town. My parents quickly made friends with the people who live next door. They've got a son of about my age. He's friendly and invites me to do things with him. But the thing is, when we see other kids, he calls them names and makes horrible comments. He wants me to join in, but I don't want to.

What can I do? If I tell my parents, it'll be hard because they really like his parents. And to be honest, I haven't got many other friends yet. If I stop hanging out with him, maybe he'll start calling me names too.

What should I do?

Alan, Salisbury

Dear Alan,

It's often difficult to make new friends when you move town, so it was almost perfect that your new neighbours had a son your age and that he wanted to be your friend. What a shame that you're finding it difficult to spend time with him.

You don't say in your letter if you think you could be friends if his behaviour was better. This is the first question you ought to ask yourself. If the answer is no, then maybe you'd better end the friendship now. Don't worry – I'm sure you'll soon make lots of friends when you start school.

However, if you think you could be friends, then you should definitely talk to him about the name-calling and explain that he had better stop saying those things. If he's going to be a good friend, he'll listen to you. If he ignores you, then this friendship probably isn't going to work.

Finally, it's a good idea to talk to your parents. They're the people who know you best and are often the best people to give you advice.

Good luck!

Susannah

Dear Susannah,

I have very bad eyesight and need to wear glasses. Because of this, some people at school call me names. I tried not to let it bother me too much, but the problem is that it happens quite often. I've always enjoyed school and had lots of friends, but I'm starting to hate going there. My grades are also getting worse and some of the teachers have said they're disappointed with me. I know I should talk to the teachers, but I'm sure this is only going to make things worse. Can you help?

Lara, Ipswich

4 DILEMMAS

READING

1 Read the definition. Then look at the pictures. What dilemmas do you think they show?

> ⊖ ▢ ⊗   ◄ ► ⌂
>
> **dilemma:** a situation in which a difficult choice has to be made between two or more alternatives

2 Read the quiz quickly. Match each picture with a question.

3 🔊 1.25 Read the quiz again and listen. Then complete it with your answers. Compare with a partner.

4 Match these responses with the quiz questions.

- [ ] **a** I'd try and fix it before she noticed.
- [ ] **b** I'd keep quiet but make sure I worked really hard for my next test.
- [ ] **c** I'd ask if I could change it for another one.
- [ ] **d** I'd write my own answer but then look at her paper to check it.
- [ ] **e** I'd ask him or her what it was about.
- [ ] **f** I'd admit I didn't have enough money and ask to borrow some from a friend.
- [ ] **g** I'd have an argument with them about it.
- [ ] **h** I'd spend some of it and give some to charity.

What would YOU do?

What would you do if ...

1 you heard a text message arrive on your girlfriend's or boyfriend's phone when he or she was out of the room?

A I wouldn't open it.

B I'd read it and pretend I hadn't.

2 you found €100 in a cash machine outside a bank?

A I'd go into the bank and give it to someone who worked there.

B I'd keep it and buy myself something nice.

3 you noticed your teacher had made a mistake marking your test and given you a better mark?

A I'd tell my teacher about the mistake immediately.

B I wouldn't say anything.

4 you broke your mum's vase while playing football in the house?

A I'd own up and say it was me.

B I'd say that the cat did it.

5 you bought a shirt, wore it to a party once and decided you didn't really like it?

A I'd give it to a friend.

B I'd take it back to the shop, say I'd never worn it and get my money back.

6 there was a party you really wanted to go to, but you thought your parents might not let you go?

A I'd be open, tell them why I wanted to go and accept their decision.

B I'd say I was staying at a friend's house, go to the party and hide the truth from them.

7 you were stuck in a difficult Maths test and noticed that you could easily copy from your friend's paper?

A I wouldn't look. I'd just try harder to answer the question myself.

B I'd look at her paper.

8 you didn't have enough money for a full-price cinema ticket?

A I'd leave and go home.

B I'd lie about my age and try and get in for a cheaper price.

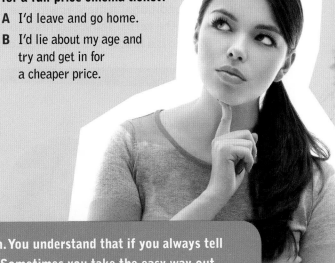

RESULTS

MORE 'A'S THAN 'B'S: You're basically an honest person. You understand that if you always tell the truth, people will trust you. **MORE 'B'S THAN 'A'S:** Sometimes you take the easy way out. Be careful because it may cause you problems. You don't want people to think of you as dishonest.

■ TRAIN TO THiNK ■

Thinking of consequences

In order to make a good decision, it's important to think of all possible consequences for others and for yourself.

5 Choose four of the questions in the quiz. Think of possible consequences for each option.

Question	Action	Consequence
1	I read the text message.	My girlfriend / boyfriend gets angry and doesn't trust me any more. We stop being friends.
	I don't read the text message.	I don't find out what the message is about.

SPEAKING

Work in pairs. Discuss these questions.

1 Which of the situations in the quiz is the most / least serious?

2 Do you agree with what the results say about you?

GRAMMAR
First and second conditional (review)

1 **Complete these sentences from the quiz on page 39 with the correct forms of the verbs. Then match them with the parts of the rule.**

1 What _____ you _____ (do) if you _____ (break) your mum's vase while playing football?

2 If you always _____ (tell) the truth, people _____ (trust) you.

> **RULE:**
> ● We use the **first conditional** to talk about real situations and their consequences. We form it with *if* + present simple / future (*will*) clause. _____
> ● We use the **second conditional** to talk about hypothetical or very unlikely situations and their outcomes. We form it with *if* + past simple / *would* clause. _____

2 **Complete the conditional sentences with the correct forms of the verbs. Think carefully about whether each one is a first or second conditional.**

What should I do?

Why is Jan so mean to me? If Jan ¹_____ (not be) so mean to me, I ²_____ (want) to invite her to my party. The problem is, she's so popular. If she ³_____ (not have) so many friends, nobody ⁴_____ (care) if she was at my party or not. I have to invite her. If I ⁵_____ (not invite) Jan to my party, nobody ⁶_____ (come) to it.

Maybe I shouldn't have a party. But if I ⁷_____ (not have) a party, I ⁸_____ (not get) any presents and I want presents! Why are birthdays always so much trouble? If it ⁹_____ (not be) my birthday next week, my life ¹⁰_____ (not be) so complicated. If I ¹¹_____ (know) what to do, I ¹²_____ (do) it. But I don't!

Workbook page 36

Time conjunctions

3 **Complete the sentences with the words.**

unless | if | until | when | as soon as

1 I don't know where he is, but I'll tell him _____ I see him.

2 I'm meeting him later, so I'll tell him _____ I see him.

3 It's really important. I'm going to tell him _____ I see him.

4 I won't tell him anything _____ he asks.

5 I'll work _____ he arrives and then I'll stop.

4 **Complete the sentences so that they are true for you. Tell your partner.**

1 As soon as I get home tonight, I …

2 If the weather is good this weekend, I …

3 When I'm 18, I …

4 Unless I get lots of homework this weekend, I …

5 I'm going to save all my money until …

Workbook page 36

VOCABULARY
Being honest

1 **Write the words in the correct columns.**

~~cheat~~ | get away with something
hide the truth | do the right thing
tell a lie | be open about something
tell the truth | own up to something

Positive behaviour	Negative behaviour
	cheat

2 **Compete the conversation with the correct form of the verbs from Exercise 1.**

DAN I've got a dilemma. The other day I ¹_____ in a test. I copied from Ben.

ANA Why?

DAN Well, I thought I could ²_____ away with it, but now the teacher wants to know who copied who.

ANA You should ³_____ up to it and say it was you.

DAN I know, but it's too difficult to ⁴_____ the truth.

ANA But you can't ⁵_____ the truth now! What about poor Ben? What were you thinking?

DAN It's Maths. I just find it so difficult.

ANA Well, you need to be ⁶_____ about this. First, say sorry for cheating and explain why you ⁷_____ a lie. Then tell your teacher what the problem is.

DAN You're right, of course. It's just so difficult to ⁸_____ the right thing sometimes.

Workbook page 38

LISTENING

1 **SPEAKING** Work in pairs. Look at the photos. What do you know about these people and characters? What difficulties might they face?

2 🔊 1.26 Listen to the conversation. What are the teenagers doing?

3 🔊 1.26 Listen again. Circle the
✳ correct answers.

1 Where are the teenagers?
   A on a long train journey
   B on the platform, waiting for a train
   C at home

2 What do they decide to play?
   A a card game invented by Maddy
   B a guessing game invented by Liam
   C a traditional children's game

3 Why isn't Andy Murray a good choice for this game?
   A Maddy and Susie don't like tennis.
   B He isn't famous enough.
   C He isn't a fictional character.

4 Why does Liam get angry when Maddy guesses Superman?
   A He chose someone too easy.
   B She doesn't let him finish.
   C She got the wrong answer.

Superman

Andy Murray

Juliet (from Romeo and Juliet)

5 Why can't Liam guess Juliet?
   A He doesn't know who Juliet is.
   B He doesn't know very much about history.
   C He gets angry with Maddy.

6 Why doesn't Maddy say 'Harry Potter' straight away?
   A She's enjoying annoying Liam.
   B She doesn't know who it is.
   C She's bored with the game.

GRAMMAR
wish and if only

1 **Read the sentences. Which fictional characters might say them? Complete the rule. Use the sentences to help you.**

1 'I wish I **could** kill Lord Voldemort.'
2 'If only our families **wouldn't** fight all the time.'
3 'I wish Lois Lane **knew** who I really was.'

> **RULE:**
> • We use *wish / if only* + the [1]_____ tense to express how we would like our current situation to be different.
> • We use *wish / if only* + [2]_____ to say that we'd like the ability or permission to do something.
> • We use *wish / if only* + [3]_____ to complain about a situation that we don't like.

> **LOOK!** We can use *was* or *were* after a singular subject (*I, he, she* or *it*) when we express wishes.
> *I wish I **was** older. / I wish I **were** older.*

2 **Complete the sentences with the correct forms of the verbs.**

see | stop | not get
not be | not fight | have

1 I wish this train journey _____ so long.
2 I wish Liam _____ talking for a while.
3 If only I _____ an interesting book with me.
4 I wish Maddy _____ with me all the time.
5 If only Maddy _____ so angry with me.
6 I wish Maddy _____ that I'm in love with her!

3 **SPEAKING** Play 'famous wishes' in groups of four.

   • Choose a famous fictional person and write three wishes. (Remember: they should be about the present situation, not the past.)
   • Read out your sentences. The other students have to guess who you are.

Workbook page 37

READING

1 **SPEAKING** Work in pairs. You find a valuable ring in the street. Think of four things you could do with it.

2 Read the story. What did Billy do with the ring?

3 Read the story again. Who do you think said these things?

1 'If only a little good luck came my way.'
2 'What's that in my cup?'
3 'I'd like to buy it.'
4 'It's a lot of money, but I can't.'
5 'I was here a few days ago.'
6 'I can't believe he didn't sell my ring!'
7 'I think that's a great idea.'
8 'We never thought we'd see you again.'

4 **SPEAKING** Work in pairs. Imagine this story is going to be made into a Hollywood film. Discuss these questions.

1 Which actors are you going to choose to play the main characters?
2 How are you going to give the film a big 'Hollywood ending'?
3 What's the title of your film?

5 Share your ideas with the class.

GRAMMAR
Third conditional (review)

1 Complete these sentences from the story with the correct forms of the verbs. Then complete the rule.

1 If Billy _____ (look) up, he _____ (see) a young lady on her way to work.
2 If he _____ (not do) the right thing, he _____ (not see) his sisters again.

> **RULE:** We use the **third conditional** to talk about situations and their outcomes in the past. We form it with:
> *if* + [1]_____ + *would(n't) have* + [2]_____ .

2 Complete the third conditional sentences.

0 If Billy *had been* on a different street, Sarah *wouldn't have seen* him.
1 Sarah _____ (see) the ring if she _____ (look) in the cup.
2 Billy _____ (keep) the ring if Sarah _____ (not return).
3 Sarah _____ (not raise) so much money if she _____ (not put) her story on the Internet.

3 Complete the sentences so that they are true for you.

1 If I hadn't gone to school today, …
2 I'd have been really happy if …
3 If I'd been born 100 years ago, …

Workbook page 37

The day Billy Ray's life changed forever

Billy Ray Harris was homeless. He spent each day on the streets of Kansas City, begging for money for food and maybe a bed for the night. Every day, as he sat thinking about his life, he occasionally heard the sound of a coin or two dropping into his cup. One day, the noise was louder than usual. If Billy had looked up, he'd have seen a young lady on her way to work. But he didn't. A little later, when he looked into the cup, he could hardly believe what he saw. At the bottom was a shining diamond ring.

Billy's first thought was to go straight to a jeweller's and that's exactly what he did. To his complete amazement, he was offered $4,000. Billy thought long and hard. Was this a mistake? It was more money than he'd seen in a long time. But then he thought about his grandfather, who had brought him up always to do the right thing, and knew he had to reconsider. His mind was made up. He'd keep the ring and maybe one day its owner would return.

In fact, he didn't have to wait long. Two days later, a young woman approached him while he was begging. She introduced herself as Sarah Darling and asked if he'd found anything unusual in his cup. Billy reached into his pocket and pulled out the ring. When he saw the smile on Sarah's face he knew he'd made the right decision. She explained that when she dropped the coins into his cup, she'd forgotten putting her ring in her purse.

VOCABULARY
Making a decision

1 Match 1–8 with the <u>underlined</u> words and phrases in the text below.

1	for a long time	5	make
2	a good	6	thought again about
3	the wrong	7	original idea
4	decide	8	made a new decision

My ᵃ<u>first thought</u> was to go with the blue. But then I thought ᵇ<u>long and hard</u> and ᶜ<u>changed my mind</u>. Maybe the red was better. But had I made ᵈ<u>the right</u> decision? Had I? I ᵉ<u>reconsidered</u> my choice. Red or blue? Red or blue? Why was it so difficult to ᶠ<u>make up my mind</u>? Well, I didn't want to make ᵍ<u>a bad</u> decision, did I? So I called my sister. Maybe she could help me ʰ<u>come to</u> a decision.

'Yes, what is it?' she asked.

'Red or blue?' I asked.

'I don't know why you're asking me,' she said. 'You only ever wear blue.'

But the story doesn't end there. Sarah told her husband the story and how she wanted to post it on the Internet. He thought it was a good idea. They also set up an online appeal to raise money for Billy. They soon had more than $185,000.

Billy Ray Harris no longer spends his days begging. He has a home and a job. The story also made the local news and he was reunited with his two sisters, who he hadn't seen for over 16 years. If he hadn't done the right thing, he wouldn't have seen his sisters again.

2 **SPEAKING** Work in pairs. Discuss these questions.

1 What's the biggest decision you've ever made?
2 Have you ever made the wrong decision? What was it?
3 How good are you at making your mind up about small things?
4 What sort of things do you usually need to think long and hard about?
5 Do you ever reconsider decisions you have made?
6 Who do you ask to help you come to important decisions?

Workbook page 38

■ THiNK VALUES ■
Doing the right thing

1 Think about a time when you had to make a difficult decision. Make notes.

1 What decision did you make?
2 What were the consequences?

2 Write a short paragraph. Include a third conditional sentence.

Last year, there was a new student in my class. Nobody wanted to sit next to him, so I did. I'm really happy I did. If I hadn't sat next to him, he wouldn't have become my best friend. What a good decision I made!

3 Read your paragraph out to the class. Then vote on the best story.

WRITING
A diary entry about a dilemma

Choose one of these situations or use your own idea. Write a diary entry about it (150–200 words). Try to use language from this unit.

1 Explain the problem.
2 Think about two possible solutions and their consequences.
3 Decide what you're going to do and why.

- You've got a detention. If you tell your parents, you won't be allowed to go to a party.
- It's your mum's birthday this weekend, but you spent all your money on clothes and haven't got any left to buy her a present.
- You saw your best friend's boyfriend / girlfriend at the cinema with another boy / girl.

And the hole gets deeper!

1 **Look at the photos and answer the questions.**

What is Jeff holding?
Who seems very interested in Mia's friend?

2 🔊 1.27 **Now read and listen to the photostory. Check your answers.**

FLORA What's with the helmet, Jeff?

JEFF It's my dad's. He does go-karting.

MIA Oh yeah, I remember now. You told us about that. He's pretty good, isn't he?

JEFF Oh yeah, he's really into it. He goes all the time now that he's got his own go-kart. Anyway, there's a problem with his helmet, so he asked me to take it to the shop.

MIA Oh, look! There's Chloë.

LEO Who's that?

MIA She's a friend of mine, from when I used to be in the orchestra.

JEFF Wow, she's pretty! If I'd known she was in the orchestra, I would have come to more concerts!

CHLOE Hi, Mia. What a nice surprise! How are you?

MIA Good, thanks, Chloë. These are my friends, Leo, Jeff and Flora.

CHLOE Hi, nice to meet you all. Hey, is that a motorbike helmet?

JEFF Well, actually, it's a go-kart helmet. It's ...

CHLOE So, you're a go-karter? Cool! I've always wanted to try go-karting!

JEFF Well, um, yes. It's just a hobby. But I race too, you know, now and again. Believe it or not, I've even won a few times.

CHLOE Wow! You actually race. That's so cool. I'd really like to try go-karting, but I've never had the chance.

JEFF Oh, that's a shame. It's good fun.

CHLOE I'm sure it is. Do you think I could ... ?

JEFF What?

CHLOE Well, I was wondering if I could come along with you sometime, maybe watch you race. Any chance?

JEFF Oh, um, well, maybe. I mean, yes, of course. That would be great.

CHLOE Cool! So, when's your next race?

JEFF Um ... Let me think. I'm not sure, to be honest.

CHLOE Well, look, when you know, call me, OK? Mia's got my number.

CHLOE Talk to you soon, I hope, Jeff. Bye, everyone!

JEFF Yeah, see you, Chloë.

FLORA Are you out of your mind? You aren't a go-karter, and just now you said you were. Why did you do that?

MIA Do you need to ask?

JEFF Well, she seemed really nice, you know, and she likes go-karting.

LEO Between you and me, I think Jeff has just dug himself into a big hole.

MIA Yes, I think you might be right. What are you going to do now, Jeff?

DEVELOPING SPEAKING

3 Work in pairs. Discuss what happens next in the story. Write down your ideas.

We think Jeff asks his dad to help him.

4 ◄ EP2 Watch and find out how the story continues.

5 Mark the sentences T (true) or F (false).

1 Jeff phones Chloë.
2 Chloë asks Jeff if he's really a go-karter.
3 Jeff goes to the go-kart track with his father.
4 Jeff makes a film of himself driving a go-kart.
5 Jeff and Chloë arrange to meet on Sunday.
6 Jeff pretends that he's hurt his knee.
7 His trick is discovered when he uses his phone.
8 Chloë never wants to see Jeff again.

PHRASES FOR FLUENCY

1 Find these expressions in the photostory. Who says them? How do you say them in your language?

1 What's with (the helmet)?
2 Believe it or not, …
3 I was wondering if …
4 Any chance?
5 Are you out of your mind?
6 Between you and me, …

2 Use the expressions in Exercise 1 to complete the conversations.

1 A Andy, _____ you could take Billy for a walk.
   B Sorry, I can't. _____, I'm really scared of dogs.
2 A Hi, Steve. Wow! _____ those really old football boots?
   B They're ancient, aren't they? _____, my dad used to wear them when he was at school. I need new ones.
3 A Hi, Jane. My phone's broken. I need to use yours. _____?
   B _____? It's brand new! I wouldn't lend it to anyone!

Pronunciation

Consonant–vowel word linking
Go to page 120. ◄))

WordWise

now

1 Look at the words and phrases in bold in these sentences from the photostory. Match them with the definitions.

1 Oh yeah, I remember **now**.
2 He goes all the time **now that** he's got his own go-kart.
3 But I race too, you know, **now and again**.
4 You aren't a go-karter, and **just now** you said you were.
5 What are you going to do **now**, Jeff?

a in the near future
b at this moment
c a moment or two ago
d because finally
e sometimes

2 Use words and phrases from Exercise 1 to complete the sentences.

1 I've finished my work, so _____ I'm going to hang out with my friends.
2 I don't listen to this music all the time, but _____ I like to play it.
3 Sally was here _____, but she's gone out.
4 I'll eat later. I'm not hungry _____.
5 I don't walk to school _____ I've got a bike.

Workbook page 38

FUNCTIONS
Apologising and accepting apologies

1 Write the expressions in the correct columns.

No problem. | I'm so sorry. | I feel awful about this. That's / It's OK. | I don't know what to say. Don't worry about it. | No worries | I'm so ashamed.

Apologising	Accepting apologies

2 Work in pairs. Imagine you're in these situations and act out conversations. Use expressions from Exercise 1.

- A has spilled a drink on B's trousers.
- A has arrived very late for a meeting with B.
- A has bumped into B and B has fallen over.
- A has completely forgotten B's name.

LISTENING
Part 1: Multiple choice

Workbook page 35

1 🔊 1.30 **You will hear people talking in eight different situations. For questions 1–8, choose the best answer (A, B or C).**

  1 You hear a boy talking about how he got his name. Why was it hard for his parents to name him?
     A They each wanted different names.
     B There weren't many possibilities for a name that worked in two languages.
     C He was born two weeks early.

  2 You hear a girl talking on her phone. What is her problem?
     A She doesn't want to invite Lucy to her birthday celebration.
     B Her mum said that Lucy can't come for a sleepover.
     C She really wants to have a big party.

  3 You hear part of an interview with a footballer. What does he find most difficult about his job?
     A not being free at weekends
     B having to work out every day
     C the comments some of the fans make

  4 You hear two friends talking about a camping trip. What advice does Alan give Steve?
     A to take a comfortable sleeping bag
     B to get a lift to the campsite
     C not to take things that weigh too much

  5 You hear a local news report. What did Clive Roberts think when he found the money?
     A I'm £10,000 richer.
     B How can I return this to the owner?
     C Could I keep this? Would anybody ever know?

  6 Two friends are talking about a party. Why did Chloë miss the party?
     A Her dad said she had to go cycling with him.
     B She fell asleep in the middle of the day.
     C She was watching TV and forgot the time.

  7 You hear a girl talking about a difficult decision. Why did she find it hard to choose which exams to take?
     A She had no idea about what career she wanted to do.
     B She didn't want to disappoint her dad.
     C She wanted to make sure her exams would help her get a well-paid job.

  8 You hear a book review on the radio. What did Carla like best about the book?
     A that she was able to understand the story
     B that it was a love story
     C the way the characters developed during the story

WRITING
Part 2: Story

Workbook page 43

2 **Your English teacher has asked you to write a short story for the school's new website. The story must begin or end with the following words:**

That name! Why did my parents give me that stupid name?!

Write your story in 140–190 words.

TEST YOURSELF

UNITS 3 & 4

VOCABULARY

1 Complete the sentences with the words / phrases in the list. There are four extra words / phrases.

brand | call | chain | cheat | consumers | get away with | image
logo | manufacturer | make | name | own up to | products | tell

1 She worked very hard for years before she started to _____ a name for herself in the theatre.
2 The company was in trouble until they started making some new _____ .
3 If you _____ during the exam, we'll take you out of the exam room and destroy your paper.
4 I like so many different kinds of music. Basically, you _____ it, I like it!
5 He tried to look at another boy's test, but the teacher saw him so he didn't _____ it.
6 I think it's so childish when you _____ other people names.
7 We didn't like our old _____ so we got a new one designed. It's on our website now.
8 Did you eat the last piece of apple pie? Come on – _____ me the truth!
9 We started with just one shop, but now we have a _____ of twenty.
10 I know you took my things without asking. Why don't you just _____ it?

/10

GRAMMAR

2 Complete the sentences with the words in the list. There are two extra words.

better | if | go | ought | unless | until | went | when

1 It's pretty late – I think I have to _____ now, OK?
2 I really wish we _____ out to eat more often.
3 I'll call you _____ the film finishes, OK?
4 I'm not going to bed _____ I finish this book – it's brilliant!
5 You'll never be his friend _____ you go and talk to him!
6 It's a secret, so you'd _____ not tell anyone else!

3 Find and correct the mistake in each sentence.

1 You shouldn't to talk to me like that. It isn't nice.
2 If they wouldn't be so expensive, I'd buy some of those chocolates.
3 I wish you don't live so far away.
4 Your eye looks bad – I think you better go to the doctor.
5 If it hadn't rained, we had gone to the beach yesterday.
6 If only we can see you more often.

/12

FUNCTIONAL LANGUAGE

4 Circle the correct words.

1 A I think we *should* / *ought* to go now.
   B That's a shame. If only you *could stay* / *stayed* a little longer.
2 A Listen, *we mustn't* / *we don't have to* miss the train tomorrow morning.
   B You're right. *I'd better not* / *I don't have to* forget to set the alarm on my phone.
3 A Hey! Stop! You *don't* / *can't* come in here. You're too young!
   B Sorry! But I really want to see the film. I wish I *would be* / *were* eighteen already!

/8

4 A Patrick *wouldn't have* / *won't have* come to the party if he'd known
     Sue was going to be there.
   B Yeah, it's a shame – if only *we'd told* / *we've told* him earlier.

MY SCORE **/30**

| 22 – 30 |
| 10 – 21 |
| 0 – 9 |

47

PRONUNCIATION

UNIT 1
Linking words with *up*

1 🔊 1.11 **Read and listen to the dialogue.**

STEVE   What's **up**, Jenny?

JENNY   I'm tired! I'**m up** late every night studying.

STEVE   You need your sleep! Can't you ge**t up** later?

JENNY   Not really. I've take**n up** the flute this year. I practise in the mornings.

STEVE   Well, it's **up** to you, but I'd give that **up**!

JENNY   Hmmm … I wish I hadn't signed **up** for the school orchestra now!

2 **What happens to the words in blue?** (Circle) **the correct word to complete the rule:**

A word ending in a *consonant / vowel* sound links with the following word when it begins with a *consonant / vowel* sound.

3 🔊 1.12 **Listen, repeat and practise.**

UNIT 2
Initial consonant clusters with /s/

1 🔊 1.14 **Read and listen to the tongue twisters.**

Strong winds **spr**ead the **sp**arks through the **str**eets.
Stella's got **str**aight hair and **str**ipes on her **sk**irt.
Stewart **spr**ayed his phone with a **sp**ecial **scr**een cleaner.

2 **Say the words in blue.**

3 🔊 1.15 **Listen, repeat and practise.**

UNIT 3
Strong and weak forms: /ɒv/ and /əv/

1 🔊 1.21 **Read and listen to the dialogue.**

JULIA   What do you always buy the same brand **of**?

JACK   I always buy the same brand **of** trainers. They're called Ace. I bought a pair **of** green ones last week.

JULIA   Ace? What are they made **of**?

JACK   They're made **of** fabric and rubber. They put a lot **of** effort into the design and quality **of** them.

JULIA   And into the marketing **of** them, too!

2 🔊 1.21 **Listen again and** underline **each of which is stressed and** (circle) **each of which is unstressed.**

3 🔊 1.22 **Listen, repeat and practise.**

UNIT 4
Consonant–vowel word linking

1 🔊 1.28 **Read and listen to the dialogue.**

LISA   I was only joking, but I wish I hadn't said it. I think she hates me.

HENRY   Well, it was unkind of you to say you didn't like her new haircut.

LISA   I know! I can't believe I said that she looked like a boy! It just came out. What should I do?

HENRY   First, I'd apologise. Then I'd admit that I prefer it long. Actually, I think she looks amazing!

2 🔊 1.28 Underline **examples of linking in the dialogue. Then listen and check.**

3 🔊 1.29 **Listen, repeat and practise.**

GET IT RIGHT!

UNIT 1
Present simple vs. present continuous

It's common to confuse the present simple and present continuous.

We use the present simple to describe facts, routine activities and opinions.

✓ I *usually go* there on foot.
✗ I'm *usually going* there on foot.

We use the present continuous to describe events that are happening now or around now.

✓ I'm *sending* you a photo of my new bike.
✗ I *send* you a photo of my new bike.

Find the error in each of these sentences. Rewrite the sentences correctly.

0   I know how hard you try to get on the team.
     I know how hard you are trying to get on
     the team.

1   I think I am the person you look for.
     _____
     _____

2   I'm playing tennis on Tuesdays.
     _____
     _____

3   At the moment I write a letter to a friend.
     _____
     _____

4   I like what you wear today.
     _____
     _____

5   I know what you mean and are appreciating your help.
     _____
     _____

6   We are playing football during most school breaks.
     _____
     _____

UNIT 2
Present perfect vs. past simple

Students often confuse the present perfect and past simple tenses.

We use the past simple when we include a past time expression to say when in the past an event took place.

✓ Yesterday I *ate* rice.
✗ Yesterday I *have eaten* rice.

We use the present perfect to talk about past events when we don't say exactly when they took place and with expressions such as *yet*, *before*, *ever* and *never*.

✓ I've never **been** to London before.
✗ I *didn't go* to London before.

Make sentences using the prompts below.

0   we / see / the advertisement at the bus stop / yesterday
     We saw the advertisement at the bus stop
     yesterday.

1   I / not see / the new Hobbit film / yet
     _____
     _____

2   you / ever / go / to Spain?
     _____
     _____

3   John / take / his exam / last week
     _____
     _____

4   Nina / get / here / a few minutes ago
     _____
     _____

5   they / not eat / at this restaurant / before
     _____
     _____

6   I / not eat / breakfast / so I'm really hungry and it's two hours till lunchtime!
     _____
     _____

Past continuous vs. past simple

> **Learners sometimes confuse the past continuous with the past simple.**
>
> ✓ I was happy when I **came** first in the race.
> ✗ I was happy when I ~~was coming~~ first in the race.

Which of these sentences are correct and which are incorrect? Rewrite the incorrect ones.

0 Last time I was visiting the library, I couldn't find the book I was looking for.
   Last time I visited the library, I couldn't find the book I was looking for.

1 When she arrived, I cooked dinner so I was a bit distracted.
   _____

2 After that, I watched TV for about an hour.
   _____

3 As usual, we were arriving at about 6 pm, then we had dinner.
   _____

4 My teacher came to see how our project went.
   _____

5 I'll never forget the time I was spending in Nepal.
   _____

6 The police saw the men and asked them what they did there.
   _____

UNIT 3
have to vs. had to

> **Learners sometimes confuse have to and had to.**
>
> **We use have to to talk about an obligation in the present, and had to to talk about an obligation in the past.**
>
> ✓ Shopping is stressful, especially if you **have to** find a particular item of clothing.
> ✗ Shopping is stressful, especially if you ~~had to~~ find a particular item of clothing.

Which of these sentences are correct and which are incorrect? Rewrite the incorrect ones.

0 The trains were fully booked so we have to forget about that trip.
   The trains were fully booked so we had to forget about that trip.

1 I'm sorry I can't attend class tomorrow because I had to go to the doctor.
   _____

2 My dad was going to work for another company so we have to move house.
   _____

3 If you want a drink after swimming, you have to go somewhere else.
   _____

4 If I have to choose between going to a small school or a large one, I would choose a large one.
   _____

5 Do we have to bring any money for the trip next week?
   _____

6 Yesterday we had to write an essay about Barack Obama.
   _____

don't have to vs. mustn't

> **Learners sometimes make errors with *don't have to* and *mustn't*.**
>
> **Although *have to* and *must* both mean something is necessary, *don't have to* means that something is <u>not necessary</u>, whereas *mustn't* means that something is <u>prohibited</u>.**
>
> ✓ I **don't have to** work tonight, as I've already finished everything.
> ✗ I ~~mustn't~~ work tonight, as I've already finished everything.
> ✓ I **mustn't** fail my exam, or I'll have to retake it.

Write the sentences with *mustn't* or *don't have to*.

0 You / stay out late or you'll be really tired tomorrow.
   You mustn't stay out late or you'll be really tired tomorrow.

1 You / finish your essay now. Mr Jenkins said that we can hand it in next Friday.
   _____

2 You / bring anything to the party – just bring yourself!
   _____

3 You / eat food in class – it's against the rules.
   _____

4 You / talk during exams.
   _____

5 You / revise every unit. The exam only includes Units 1 to 3.
   _____

6 You / use your phone in class. It'll be confiscated.
   _____

UNIT 4
if vs. *when*

Learners often confuse *if* with *when*.

We use *if* to indicate possible actions or events.

✓ *It'll be best for us **if** everyone goes by bicycle. Car parking facilities are limited.*
✗ *It'll be best for us ~~when~~ everyone goes by bicycle. Car parking facilities are limited.*

We use *when* to indicate events which have happened in the past or are going to happen in the future.

✓ *I can pass on your message. I'll tell him **when** I see him tomorrow.*
✗ *I can pass on your message. I'll tell him **if** I see him tomorrow.*

Complete these sentences with *if* or *when*.

0   I was very pleased _*when*_ I read your letter.
1   I had a great time _____ I went to New York.
2   Would it be OK _____ I invited my friend?
3   I'll call you _____ I get home tonight.
4   Do you mind _____ we meet at 5.00 instead of 4.00?
5   _____ you're free on Saturday, come to the cinema with us!
6   He went to Africa _____ he was 21 because of his job.
7   How much would it cost _____ we were a group of ten?

STUDENT A

Student A

You aren't very happy with your brother or sister. He/She plays loud music that you don't like when you're trying to work. He/She doesn't even keep the door closed. What else upsets you about this? You have decided to talk to him/her about it. Try and use the expressions in Exercise 1.

Excuse me, [name], I need a word ...

UNIT 1, PAGE 19

Student B

You aren't very happy with your brother or sister. He/She keeps taking your clothes without asking you. He/She makes a real mess when he/she takes them from your wardrobe. What else upsets you about this? You have decided to talk to him/her about it. Try and use the expressions in Exercise 1.

Excuse me, [name], I need a word ...

Acknowledgements

The authors and publishers acknowledge the following sources of copyright material and are grateful for the permissions granted. While every effort has been made, it has not always been possible to identify the sources of all the material used, or to trace all copyright holders. If any omissions are brought to our notice, we will be happy to include the appropriate acknowledgements on reprinting.

Cambridge University Press for the text on p. 36 excerpted from *Wild Country* by Margaret Johnson. Copyright © 2008 Cambridge University Press. Reproduced with permission of Cambridge University Press. All rights reserved;

The Independent for the text on p. 42 adapted from 'Luck Changes for Billy Ray Harris, the homeless man who returned an engagement ring dropped into his beggar's cup' by David Usborne, *The Independent* 25.03.13. © Independent Print Limited, David Usborne, Independent Online. Reproduced with permission. All rights reserved;

The publishers are grateful to the following for permission to reproduce copyright photographs and material:

T = Top, B = Below, L = Left, R = Right, C = Centre, B/G – Background

p. 4: ©Ermolaev Alexander/Shutterstock; p. 5 (B/G): ©Triff/Shutterstock; p. 5 (R): ©Robin Marchant/Getty Images; p. 6 (L): ©Jubilee Images/Alamy; p. 6 (C): ©Nickolay Khoroshkov/Shuttersock; p. 6 (R): ©Richard Coombs/Alamy; p. 7: ©dwphotos/Shutterstock; p. 8: ©Tetra Images/Alamy; p. 9: ©Stewart Cook/REX; p. 11 (T, C): ©cobalt88/Shutterstock; p. 11 (B): ©artjazz/Shutterstock; p. 12 (C): ©Jacek Chabraszewski/iStock/Getty Images Plus/Getty Images; p. 12 (TL): ©Olaf Speier/Shutterstock; p. 12 (R, BL): ©Sean Justice/The Image Bank/Getty Images; p. 13: ©Ben Welsh/Corbis; p. 15 (L): ©David Fisher/REX; p. 15 (C): ©UNITED ARTISTS/THE KOBAL COLLECTION; p. 15 (R): ©Lipnitzki/Roger Viollet/Getty Images; p. 16 (B/G): ©Ensuper/Shutterstock; p. 16 (R): ©Jim Craigmyle/Corbis; p. 20 (L): ©The Art Archive/Alamy; p. 20 (R): ©Monkey Business Images/Shutterstock; p. 21: ©GL Archive/Alamy; p. 22: ©eelnosiva/iStock/Getty Images Plus/Getty Images; p. 24 (TR): ©The Art Archive/Alamy; p. 24 (BL): ©Classic Image/Alamy; p. 24 (B/G): ©RoyStudio.eu/Shutterstock; p. 25 (T): ©Roland Kemp/Dorling Kindersley/Getty Images; p. 25 (B): ©Dmitry Naumov/iStock/Getty Images Plus/Getty Images; p. 26 (TR): ©PavelSvoboda/Shutterstock; p. 26 (BL):

©Steven Kazlowski/Science Faction/Getty Images; p. 26 (B/G): ©Rigamondis/Shutterstock; p. 27: ©Agencja Fotograficzna Caro/Alamy; p. 28: ©Accord/Shutterstock; p. 30 (TL): ©Swatch; p. 30 (TR): ©WhatsApp; p. 30 (BL): ©Jaguar; p. 30 (BR): ©Pret A Manger; p. 30-31 (B/G): ©POMACHKA/iStock/Getty Images Plus/Getty Images; p. 32: ©Kevin Dodge/Corbis; p. 33: ©Beau Lark/Corbis; p. 34 (TL): ©Alberto E. Rodriguez/Getty Images; p. 34 (TR): ©REX; p. 34 (B): ©roundstripe/Shutterstock; p. 36 (TR): ©nito/Shutterstock; p. 36 (C): Complete front cover: *Wild Country* Level 3 Lower Intermediate (2008) by Margaret Johnson 978-0-521-71367-2. Reproduced with permission of Cambridge University Press; p. 36 (B/G): ©Anneka/Shutterstock; p. 37: ©wavebreakmedia/Shutterstock; p. 39 (B/G): ©happykanppy/Shutterstock; p. 39 (BR): ©shvili/iStock/Getty Images Plus/Getty Images; p. 40: ©Martin Novak/Shutterstock; p. 41 (L): ©Yunus Kaymaz/Anadolu Agency/Getty Images; p. 41 (C): ©WARNER BROS/THE KOBAL COLLECTION;
p. 41 (R): ©AMBER ENTERTAINMENT/ECHO LAKE PRODUCTIONS/INDIANA PRODUCTION COMPANY/SWAROVASKI ENTERTAINMENT/THE KOBAL COLLECTION; p. 42-43 (B/G): ©Pawel Gaul/E+/Getty Images; p. 43: ©Feng Yu/Shutterstock.

Commissioned photography by: Jon Barlow p. 18, 44

Cover photographs by: (L): ©Andrea Haase/iStock/Getty Images Plus/Getty Images; (TR): ©Stephen Moore/Digital Vision Vectors/Getty Images; (BR): ©Pete Starman/Stone/Getty Images.

The publishers are grateful to the following illustrators: Bryan Beach (Advocate Art) 10, 31, 43; David Semple 17, 35; Graham Kennedy 23; Julian Mosedale 38

The publishers are grateful to the following contributors: Blooberry: text design and layouts; Claire Parson: cover design; Hilary Fletcher: picture research; Leon Chambers: audio recordings; Silversun Media Group: video production; Karen Elliott: Pronunciation sections; Matt Norton: Get it right! sections

WORKBOOK 3A

Herbert Puchta, Jeff Stranks & Peter Lewis-Jones

B1+

CAMBRIDGE
UNIVERSITY PRESS

Acknowledgements

The authors and publishers acknowledge the following sources of copyright material and are grateful for the permissions granted. While every effort has been made, it has not always been possible to identify the sources of all the material used, or to trace all copyright holders. If any omissions are brought to our notice, we will be happy to include the appropriate acknowledgements on reprinting.

Corpus

Development of this publication has made use of the Cambridge English Corpus (CEC). The CEC is a computer database of contemporary spoken and written English, which currently stands at over one billion words. It includes British English, American English and other varieties of English. It also includes the Cambridge Learner Corpus, developed in collaboration with Cambridge English Language Assessment. Cambridge University Press has built up the CEC to provide evidence about language use that helps to produce better language teaching materials.

English Profile

This product is informed by the English Vocabulary Profile, built as part of English Profile, a collaborative programme designed to enhance the learning, teaching and assessment of English worldwide. Its main funding partners are Cambridge University Press and Cambridge English Language Assessment and its aim is to create a 'profile' for English linked to the Common European Framework of Reference for Languages (CEF). English Profile outcomes, such as the English Vocabulary Profile, will provide detailed information about the language that learners can be expected to demonstrate at each CEF level, offering a clear benchmark for learners' proficiency. For more information, please visit www.englishprofile.org

Cambridge Dictionaries

Cambridge dictionaries are the world's most widely used dictionaries for learners of English. The dictionaries are available in print and online at dictionary.cambridge.org. Copyright © Cambridge University Press, reproduced with permission.

The publishers are grateful to the following for permission to reproduce copyright photographs and material:

T = Top, B = Below, L = Left, R = Right, C = Centre

p. 48: ©KIM NGUYEN/Shutterstock; p. 50: ©Lebrecht Music and Arts Photo Library/Alamy; p. 51: 'The Boy Who Biked the World' 'On the Road to Africa' (part 1) (Nov 2011). Published by Eye Books. Used with permission; p. 58: ©Bobby Bank/WireImage/Getty Images; p. 59 (TL): ©sauletas/Shutterstock; p. 59 (TC): ©Neirfy/Shutterstock; p. 59 (TR): ©Ryan DeBerardinis/Shutterstock; p. 59 (BL): ©Vladimir Caplinskij/Shutterstock; p. 59 (BC): ©SUSUMU NISHINAGA/SCIENCE PHOTO LIBRARY; p. 59 (BR): ©Lourens Smak/Alamy; p. 68: ©Rawpixel/Shutterstock; p. 69 (T): ©Jeremy Horner/Alamy; p. 69 (CL): ©HLPhoto/Shutterstock; p. 69 (CR): ©REX; p. 69 (B): ©ROMEO GACAD/AFP/Getty Images; p. 76: ©David Young-Wolff/The Image Bank/Getty Images; p. 78: ©Clarissa Leahy/Cultura/Getty Images; p. 83: ©Blend Images/Shutterstock; p. 86: ©Jarno Gonzalez Zarraonandia/Shutterstock; p. 87: ©Mary Evans Picture Library/Alamy; p. 89: ©Fulcanelli/Shutterstock; p. 90: ©Air Images/Shutterstock; p. 94: ©PjrStudio/Alamy; p. 98 (TL): ©Bragin Alexey/Shutterstock; p. 98 (TR): ©Julian Rovagnati/Shutterstock; p. 98 (BL): ©Robyn Mackenzie/Shutterstock; p. 98 (BR): ©Ivonne Wierink/Shutterstock; p. 99: ©Taina Sohlman/Shutterstock; p. 104: ©Neil Bradfield/Shutterstock; p. 105: ©KPA/Zuma/REX; p. 106: ©Paul Bradbury/Caiaimage/Getty Images; p. 109: ©Lisa Peardon/The Image Bank/Getty Images; p. 112 (L): ©Photo File/MLB Photos via Getty Images; p. 112 (R): ©Jon Kopaloff/FilmMagic/Getty Images; p. 113: ©Juanmonino/iStock/Getty Images Plus.

Cover photographs by: (TR): ©Stephen Moore/Digital Vision Vectors/Getty Images; (L): ©Andrea Haase/iStock/Getty Images Plus/Getty Images; (BR): ©Pete Starman/Stone/Getty Images.

The publishers are grateful to the following illustrators:

Bryan Beach (Advocate Art) 34
David Semple 7, 28, 39, 42
Fred van Deelen (The Organisation) 20
Julian Mosedale 11, 36

The publishers are grateful to the following contributors:

Blooberry: text design and layouts; Claire Parson: cover design; Hilary Fletcher: picture research; Leon Chambers: audio recordings; Karen Elliott: Pronunciation sections; Matt Norton: Get it right! exercises

CONTENTS

WELCOME

A MUSIC MAKERS
be allowed to / let

1 Rewrite the sentences using the word in brackets.

House rules: what my parents let or don't let me do.

0 My parents don't let me play loud music in my bedroom. (allowed)

  I'm not allowed to play loud music in my bedroom.

1 My parents let me stay up late at the weekend. (allowed)

  _____

2 I'm allowed to practise my electric guitar in the garage. (let)

  _____

3 I'm not allowed go out on school nights. (let)

  _____

4 My parents let me have parties at home. (allowed)

  _____

5 I'm not allowed to go to concerts on my own. (let)

  _____

Music

1 Unscramble the words and write them in the correct list. Add two more items to each list.

srumd | laslacsic | jzaz | oilniv
tagriu | opp | inapo | par

Musical instruments	Types of music
_____	_____
_____	_____
_____	_____
_____	_____
_____	_____

2 Complete the sentences so they are true for you.

1 I really like listening to _____

2 I never listen to _____

3 I play _____

4 I'd love to play _____

Verbs of perception

1 Complete with the correct form of the verbs in brackets.

1 Why _____ you _____ (smell) the milk?

2 What's for dinner? It _____ (smell) great.

3 What _____ you _____ (look) at?

4 You _____ (not look) great. What's the matter?

5 It _____ (taste) awful. What is it?

6 Why _____ you _____ (taste) the soup again?

7 **A** Why _____ you _____ my coat (feel)?

   B I'm sorry. It's just so soft.

8 I like the way this jumper _____ (feel) .

9 I love your new hairstyle. It _____ (look) fantastic!

10 Your hands _____ (feel) very cold. Are you OK?

11 She's _____ (not taste) the food for the wedding today; she'll do it tomorrow.

12 I don't like that new building. It really _____ (not look) good.

Big screen, small screen

1 Do the word puzzle and find the name of the biggest film of 1997.

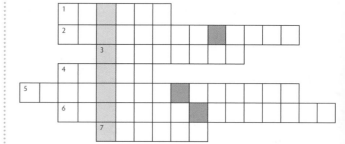

1 A film that is full of explosions and car chases.

2 A cartoon style film, usually for children.

3 An exciting film full of suspense.

4 A film with a powerful story.

5 A film that makes you laugh and maybe cry.

6 A film about other worlds.

7 A film that makes you laugh.

Present perfect tenses

1 Circle the correct form of the verb.

1 I haven't *watched* / *been watching* TV for more than a week.

2 I've *seen* / *been seeing* this film before.

3 The cinema has *shown* / *been showing* the same film for weeks now.

4 If you've *lost* / *been losing* your ticket, you can't come in.

5 They've *waited* / *been waiting* in the cinema queue for three hours.

6 You've *read* / *been reading* the TV guide for an hour. Can I have a look now?

TV programmes

1 Match the parts to make types of TV programme.

0	chat	com
1	game	programme
2	drama	show
3	sit	news
4	sports	show
5	the	series

SUMMING UP

1 Complete the conversation with the words in the list. There are three you won't use.

're watching | let | 've been watching | the news
jazz | allowed to | watch | to watch | watched
've watched | guitar | drama series

DANNY Ben, it's my turn ¹_____ TV.

BEN Just give me twenty more minutes.

DANNY But you ²_____ TV for more than two hours now. You're not even ³_____ watch so much TV. Does Mum know?

BEN Yes, she does. Anyway I'm almost finished.

DANNY Yes but I want to watch ⁴_____ and it starts in five minutes.

BEN You can ⁵_____ it later. I really need to see the end of this.

DANNY What is it that you ⁶_____ anyway?

BEN CrimeWave

DANNY What, that American ⁷_____?

BEN Yes, that's the one. It's the last episode in the series. I can't miss it. I ⁸_____ all the others. I want to know how it ends.

DANNY I'll tell you how it ends. The policeman's the murderer. Now ⁹_____ me watch my show.

B TIME TO ACT
The environment

1 🔊02 Complete the sentences with the words in the list. Then listen and check.

smog | flooding | global warming
pollution | fumes | litter

1 With the Earth's temperature rising each year, many scientists now believe _____ is the biggest threat to our planet.

2 _____ from factories and cars are creating huge _____ problems and many of the world's largest cities are permanently covered by thick _____ .

3 There has been serious _____ across the area and many people have had to leave their homes.

4 I get so angry when I see people dropping _____ in the streets. Why can't they use the bins?

Question tags

1 Match the sentences and the tags.

1 You don't care about the environment, ☐

2 You campaign for the environment, ☐

3 Global warming is getting serious, ☐

4 The world's not going to end tomorrow, ☐

5 You didn't go on the protest march, ☐

6 You threw your rubbish in the bin, ☐

7 The Earth can't take much more, ☐

8 Science can find a solution, ☐

a	isn't it?	e	didn't you?
b	did you?	f	do you?
c	can it?	g	is it?
d	can't it?	h	don't you?

2 Complete with the correct question tags.

1 You're from Argentina, _____ ?

2 This is pretty easy, _____ ?

3 You know him, _____ ?

4 They played really well, _____ ?

5 They don't speak English, _____ ?

6 She's working in London now, _____ ?

7 He can't sing, _____ ?

8 He won't be late, _____ ?

9 You've been to Canada, _____ ?

10 I shouldn't have said that, _____ ?

Party time

1 Match the sentence halves.

Am I ready for the party? Well, so far …

1 I haven't found anywhere ☐
2 I haven't got permission ☐
3 I haven't drawn up ☐
4 So clearly I haven't sent out ☐
5 I haven't hired ☐
6 Or even got the money to pay ☐
7 I haven't decorated ☐
8 And I haven't organised ☐

a the guest list.
b the food.
c a DJ.
d a deposit for one.
e the room.
f from Mum and Dad.
g to have a party.
h any invitations.

Am I ready? Nearly.

Indefinite pronouns

1 Complete the sentences with the words in the list.

everything | something | everyone | nowhere
somewhere | anyone | no one | nothing

The party was terrible.

1 I didn't know _____ .
2 _____ I tried to speak to just ignored me.
3 There was _____ to eat at all.
4 You had to pay for a drink and _____ on the menu was really expensive.
5 I wanted to leave my coat _____ but there was no cloakroom.
6 It was so crowded there was _____ to sit.
7 I wanted _____ to do so I went to the dance floor.
8 But _____ wanted to dance with me.

Arranging a party

1 Complete the conversation with the words in the list. There are two you won't use.

something | everywhere | sent out
decorating | everyone | get | anyone
everything | hiring | nowhere
organising | anything

POPPY So, Jake, is [1]_____ ready for the party tomorrow?

JAKE I think so. I've just finished [2]_____ the room and [3]_____ the food.

POPPY So there will be [4]_____ to eat?

JAKE Yes, and to drink.

POPPY So who's coming? [5]_____ I know?

JAKE There'll be loads of people you know. I [6]_____ about 30 invitations.

POPPY That's a lot of people. Did you have to [7]_____ permission from your parents?

JAKE Of course, I'm having the party at our house.

POPPY Is there [8]_____ I can do?

JAKE Well, you could bring some music with you. I'm not [9]_____ a DJ.

POPPY OK, I'll bring some music that will get [10]_____ dancing.

SUMMING UP

1 ◀))03 Put the dialogue in order. Listen and check.

☐ **BOB** Of course there is. I'm organising a protest march for Sunday. Do you want to join me?

☐ **BOB** That's a shame. But you could donate a bit of money, couldn't you?

☐ **BOB** And I don't think the government will do anything about it.

☐ **BOB** And that is why I think we should do something about it.

☐1☐ **BOB** I think the pollution in our city is getting worse each year.

☐ **SUE** I'm afraid I left my wallet at home. Sorry.

☐ **SUE** So do I. It's a real problem, isn't it?

☐ **SUE** Neither do I. They never do.

☐ **SUE** But there's nothing we can do, is there?

☐ **SUE** I'd love to but I can't. I'm busy.

C A BIT OF ADVICE
Health

1 Match the sentence halves.

1 Take this medicine and you'll feel
2 I always get
3 Dad's going to hospital to have
4 Can you phone the doctor and make
5 Why don't you see
6 You need to take more

a sick when I travel by car.
b an appointment for me?
c a doctor about your headaches?
d exercise to lose some weight.
e better in half an hour.
f an operation next week.

2 Complete the sentences with the correct form of the phrases in the list.

take some exercise | feel sick | have an operation | make an appointment | get better | see a doctor

1 I hope you _____ soon.

2 Hello, I'd like to _____ with Dr. Hill.

3 He's _____ .

4 I think you need to _____ .

3 That dog needs to _____ .

6 I _____ !

Giving advice

1 Complete the advice with the missing words.

> I get really tired when I have to run.

1 You _____ take more exercise.
2 You _____ better see a doctor.
3 You _____ to lose some weight.
4 You should _____ eat so much.
5 You had _____ be careful.
6 You ought _____ join a gym.

2 Write one piece of advice for each of these people.

1 'I can't do my homework.'

_____

2 'I'm bored.'

_____

3 'I haven't got any money.'

_____

4 'I'm new at school and I don't know anyone.'

_____

Comparisons

1 **Use the words in brackets and any other necessary words to complete the sentences.**

1 The Oscars are _____ (important) award ceremony in the film industry.

2 The host wasn't _____ (funny) the guy who did it last year.

3 The ceremony was a lot _____ (long).

4 The best actor's speech was _____ (bad) I can remember.

5 However, I think the actors were dressed _____ (beautiful) than usual.

6 Apparently one actress was wearing _____ (expensive) dress in the world.

2 **Rewrite the sentences so that they mean the same thing.**

1 It's hotter today than it was yesterday.

Yesterday wasn't _____

2 I've never seen a more boring film in my life.

That was _____

3 She's the kindest person I know.

I don't anyone as _____

4 I used to remember things more easily when I was younger.

I don't _____

5 Martin and Steve play tennis equally as well.

Steve plays tennis _____

6 It's the most expensive car in the world.

There isn't a car as _____

SUMMING UP

1 ◀))04 **Put the dialogue in order. Listen and check.**

☐ BRIAN I'm going to. I've made an appointment.

☐ BRIAN I'm not sure. Every day I wake up more tired than the day before.

☐ BRIAN I know. I'm not sure I can wait that long.

☐1 BRIAN I've been feeling really sick recently.

☐ BRIAN The problem is it's for next Thursday. They didn't have one any earlier.

☐ VICKY Oh dear. What's wrong?

☐ VICKY You'd better call them and tell them it's an emergency.

☐ VICKY What! That's a week from now.

☐ VICKY Sick and tired. You should see a doctor.

☐ VICKY Well hopefully he'll be able to help you get better.

D HELP!
Sequencing words

1 **Rearrange the letters to make four sequencing words.**

1 rafte _____

2 hent _____

3 yanllif _____

4 ta rifts _____

2 **Use the words in Exercise 1 to complete the story.**

1 _____ we thought we'd never get out. The door just wouldn't open.

2 _____ five minutes of kicking the door, we were exhausted.

3 _____ Dad found the key in his pocket.

4 _____ we got the door open.

Reported speech

1 **Report the conversation.**

0 JILL I need help.

1 SUE What's the matter?

2 JILL I can't find my key.

3 SUE Check inside your pocket.

4 JILL I've already done that.

5 SUE Have you checked the door?

6 JILL Why do you want me to do that?

7 SUE That's where you always leave them.

0 *Jill said that she needed help.*

1 Sue asked Jill _____

_____

2 Jill said that _____

_____

3 Sue told Jill _____

_____

4 Jill said _____

_____

5 Sue asked Jill _____

_____

6 Jill asked Sue _____

_____

7 Sue said _____

Asking for and offering help

1 Complete the words in the sentences.

1 Have you got a f_____ m_____?

2 C_____ I help you?

3 Can you l_____ me a h_____?

4 Could you h_____ me with something?

5 Do you n_____ any help?

2 Put the dialogue in order.

☐ MIMI I said that I was going to tidy it after I'd done my homework.

☐ MIMI What deal?

☐ MIMI Could you help me with my homework?

☐ MIMI That's the same deal we had before!

☐ MIMI But you said you'd help me.

☐1 MIMI Dad, have you got a few minutes?

☐ DAD Tidy your room and then I'll lend you a hand with your homework.

☐ DAD And you said you'd tidy your room – remember?

☐ DAD That depends. What do you want?

☐ DAD I'm sorry but I'm a bit busy.

☐ DAD So I'll make you a deal.

IT vocabulary

1 Match the sentence halves.

1 Have you seen that Brian has posted ☐

2 Before you start you have to key ☐

3 I'm having a problem installing ☐

4 Send me the photo. You can attach ☐

5 I'm going to upload ☐

6 I'm sorry. I deleted your ☐

7 I'm not sure how to activate ☐

8 It's taking ages to download ☐

a all my holiday photos online.

b message. Can you send it again?

c the flight mode on this tablet.

d this program. Can you help?

e this file. It's really big.

f another message on the school website?

g it to an email.

h in your password.

Passive tenses

1 Rewrite the sentences using the passive.

1 Five people have posted new messages on my website.

Five new messages _____

2 Someone uploaded the video onto YouTube.

The video _____

3 Someone had already keyed in my password.

My password _____

4 Two million people have downloaded this video.

This video _____

5 No one activated the flight mode.

The flight mode _____

6 The program is attaching the file to the message.

The file _____

SUMMING UP

1 Complete the dialogue with words in the list.

files | said I | buy | has accessed | said he
passwords | has been | delete | installed
is being | then

LIAM My computer [1]_____ hacked.

KATE What do you mean, 'hacked'?

LIAM Someone [2]_____ my computer from another computer.

KATE Really? How do you know?

LIAM A program has been [3]_____ that has deleted loads of my [4]_____ .

KATE That's terrible.

LIAM And all my [5]_____ have been stolen too.

KATE So what are you going to do?

LIAM My computer [6]_____ looked at by an expert at the moment. He [7]_____ could hopefully [8]_____ the program.

KATE And if he can't?

LIAM He [9]_____ 'd have to buy new computer.

KATE Well, if you do, remember to [10]_____ some antivirus software.

LIAM Yes, and [11]_____ create some new passwords!

1 LIFE PLANS

GRAMMAR

Present tenses (review) `SB page 14`

1 ★☆☆ **What tense? Write PS (present simple) PC (present continuous) PPS (present perfect simple) or PPC (present perfect continuous).**

0 I <u>haven't decided</u> what I want to do yet.   *PPS*

1 I always <u>do</u> my homework when I get home from school.   ____

2 Liam <u>hasn't been doing</u> well at school for a few months.   ____

3 My sister<u>'s always talking</u> on her phone.   ____

4 They<u>'ve been thinking</u> about buying a new house for more than a year now.   ____

5 Jim<u>'s forgotten</u> to do his homework again.   ____

6 Steve <u>doesn't want</u> to go to university next year.   ____

7 It's the last week of term so we<u>'re not doing</u> very much at school.   ____

2 ★★☆ **Complete the sentences with the words in the list.**

've been writing | don't write | 've played
's playing | hasn't been playing | plays
haven't written | 'm writing

1 No, he's not busy. He _____ cards on the computer.

2 I _____ my party invitations. Who should I invite?

3 Most people _____ letters, just emails.

4 I _____ all morning. My hand's tired.

5 My cousin usually _____ tennis twice a day. He loves it.

6 I _____ to thank my aunt for my present yet. I must do it tonight.

7 We _____ all of these games. Have you got any others?

8 She's not very good at the piano. She _____ for very long.

3 ★★☆ (Circle) **the correct words.**

We [1]*do / 're doing* some really important exams at school over the next few weeks so I [2]*spend / 'm spending* most of my free time studying for them at the moment. Normally the two things I [3]*like / 'm liking* most in life are TV and computer games but I [4]*don't watch / 'm not watching* any TV and I [5]*don't play / 'm not playing* computer games while the exams are on. I usually [6]*help / am helping* my dad in the shop at the weekends. He [7]*doesn't pay / isn't paying* me a lot but I [8]*like / 'm liking* getting the money. I [9]*don't work / 'm not working* there for a while. I [10]*need / 'm needing* the time for revision.

4 ★★☆ **Complete the conversations. Use the present perfect simple or continuous.**

1 A You look tired, Paula.
   B I am. I _____ very well lately. (not sleep)

2 A _____ your homework? (finish)
   B Nearly.

3 A Where's Bob?
   B I don't know. I _____ him for a few hours. (not see)

4 A You're dirty. What _____ ? (do)
   B Helping Mum in the garden.

5 ★★★ **Complete the conversation with the verb in brackets. Use present simple, present continuous, present perfect simple or present perfect continuous.**

JULES   [0] *Have* you *seen* (see) Tara recently? I [1] _____ (not see) her for weeks.

DAN   No, but she [2] _____ (text) me most days.

JULES   So what [3] _____ (do) these days?

DAN   Well, she [4] _____ (train) really hard for the past month.

JULES   Training? For what?

DAN   She [5] _____ (want) to be a professional footballer. Chelsea football club [6] _____ (invite) her to train with them. She starts with them on Monday.

Future tense (review) SB page 15

6 ★★☆ Look at Gillian's diary and write sentences about her plans for next week. Use the present continuous.

Monday	am: fly to Madrid pm: have meeting with Paulo
Tuesday	am: take train to Barcelona pm: watch football match at Camp Nou stadium
Wednesday	am: fly back to London

0 On Monday morning *she's flying to Madrid.*
1 On Monday afternoon _____
2 On Tuesday morning _____
3 On Tuesday afternoon _____
4 On Wednesday morning _____

7 ★★☆ Complete the sentences. Use a verb from the list and the correct form of *going to*. Then match them to the pictures.

~~see~~ | not visit | study | move | not ski | make

0 We *'re going to see* _____ a play tonight. I've got the tickets.
1 The car's broken down. We _____ Grandma today.
2 I _____ a curry tonight. I've just bought all the ingredients.
3 Sue _____ Maths at Bristol University in September.
4 Paul has hurt his leg. He _____ today.
5 They are selling their house. They _____ to London.

8 ★★☆ Read the sentences. Write A for an arrangement, P for a prediction or I for an intention.

0 I've got a tennis lesson at 10 o'clock. `A`
1 I phoned the dentist and made an appointment to see him this afternoon. ☐
2 People living on the moon one day? Yes, definitely. ☐
3 We've decided where to stay in London – the Ritz hotel. ☐
4 I've decided what to do next year – travel around the world. ☐
5 My dad, let me go to the party? No way! ☐

9 ★★★ Rewrite the sentences in Exercise 8 using the correct future tense.

0 *I'm playing tennis at 10 o'clock.*
1 _____
2 _____
3 _____
4 _____
5 _____

10 ★★★ What do you think your life will be like when you are 30?

1 (be married) _____
2 (have children) _____
3 (live in a different country) _____

GET IT RIGHT!

will vs. present continuous

Learners often use *will* + infinitive where the present continuous is needed.

✓ *I'm seeing the dentist because my tooth is hurting.*
✗ ~~I'll see~~ *the dentist because my tooth is hurting.*
✓ *I'm not sure we***'ll get** *it done in time.*
✗ *I'm not sure we're getting it done in time.*

Complete the sentences with a verb from the list in the correct form.

~~come~~ | win | see | go | not go | have (x2)

0 It's good that you *are coming* to see me in Brazil!
1 We _____ a party next weekend – do you want to come?
2 I think Real Madrid _____ tonight.
3 My brother _____ to university next week. He's packing at the moment.
4 I _____ to his party later because I have to study for tomorrow's exam.
5 We think you _____ a great time on holiday.
6 Maybe I _____ you there.

VOCABULARY

Making changes

make a resolution
give (something) up
do well
struggle with (something)
take (something) up
break a bad habit
form a good habit
change your ways

Life plans

leave school
get a degree
travel the world
start a career
get promoted
settle down
start a family
retire

Phrases with *up*

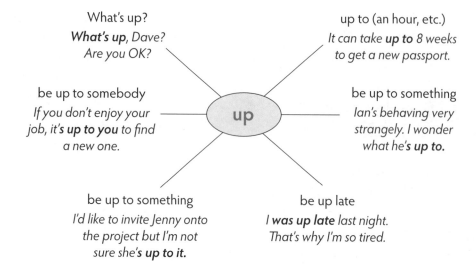

What's up?
What's up, Dave?
Are you OK?

up to (an hour, etc.)
*It can take **up to** 8 weeks*
to get a new passport.

be up to somebody
If you don't enjoy your
*job, it's **up to you** to find*
a new one.

be up to something
Ian's behaving very
strangely. I wonder
*what he's **up to**.*

be up to something
I'd like to invite Jenny onto
the project but I'm not
*sure she's **up to it**.*

be up late
*I **was up late** last night.*
That's why I'm so tired.

Key words in context

arrangement	Who made all the **arrangements** for the party?
blame	Don't **blame** me for getting here late. I said we should take a taxi.
careers advisor	The **careers advisor** told me I should think about a job in politics.
criticise	Why do you always **criticise** everything I do? Do I never do anything right?
earn a living	He **earns a living** helping the elderly.
good intentions	He had a lot of **good intentions** at the start of the year but unfortunately he forgot most of them.
intention	I'm sorry I said that. It was never my **intention** to upset you.
leave (something) to the last minute	Maybe if you didn't always **leave your homework to the last minute**, you'd get better marks for it.
lifestyle	He has a very interesting **lifestyle**. He lives half the year in France and the rest in the USA.
prediction	I'm not going to make a **prediction** about this world cup because I think lots of teams could win it.
translator	My uncle is a **translator** at the United Nations. He speaks six languages.

Making changes `SB page 14`

1 ★☆☆ **Match the sentence halves.**

1 I've decided not to make ☐
2 I'm trying to give ☐
3 He's on a diet and doing ☐
4 I'm trying to get fitter but I'm struggling ☐
5 I need a new hobby so I've taken ☐
6 It's hard to break ☐
7 It's important for kids to form ☐
8 My dad needs to eat better but he's never going to change ☐

a really well. He's lost 5 kg already.
b with getting myself to the gym every day.
c good habits.
d his ways.
e up photography.
f up eating chocolate but it's so difficult.
g any resolutions this year.
h a habit sometimes.

2 ★★★ **Write down:**

1 a resolution you'd like to make for next year.
_____
2 something you'd like to give up.
_____
3 a school subject you do well in.
_____
4 a school subject you struggle with.
_____
5 a new hobby you'd like to take up.
_____
6 a bad habit you'd like to break.

Life plans `SB page 17`

3 ★★☆ **Read the definitions and write the words and expressions.**

1 t_____ t_____ w_____ : go out and see other countries
2 g_____ p_____ : be given a better job (usually in the same company)
3 l_____ s_____ : finish compulsory education
4 r_____ : finish your professional life
5 g_____ a d_____ : graduate from university
6 s_____ d_____ : get married, buy a house, etc.
7 s_____ a f_____ : have children
8 s_____ a c_____ : begin your professional life

4 ★★☆ **Complete the sentences with the words and phrases from Exercise 3.**

1 My brother just loves being free. I can't see him ever wanting to _____ .
2 It's not easy to _____ a new _____ when you're 50.
3 The government wants to raise the age that you can _____ to 18.
4 I certainly want to _____ one day. I'd like at least three children.
5 I want to take a few years off work and _____ . I'd love to spend some time in Asia.
6 These days many people can't afford to _____ before they're 70.
7 I _____ from university but I've never really used it in my professional life.
8 If you work hard, you might _____ to junior manager next year.

WordWise `SB page 19`
Phrases with *up*

5 ★★☆ **Put the sentences in the correct order.**

☐ LINDA Why didn't you just go to bed?
☐ LINDA Really? What were you <u>up to</u>?
☐ LINDA Why? I don't understand.
1 LINDA <u>What's up</u>, Sam?
☐ SAM I was just playing video games with my dad. We were <u>up</u> until 1 am.
☐ SAM Well we were playing on the TV in my bedroom!
☐ SAM Nothing. I'm just feeling a bit tired. I was <u>up late</u>.
☐ SAM I wanted to but it wasn't <u>up to me</u>. I had to wait for my dad to finish.

6 ★★☆ **Match the underlined words in Exercise 5 with their meanings.**

1 doing _____
2 awake _____
3 didn't go to bed early _____
4 the matter _____
5 my decision / choice _____

Pronunciation
Linking words with *up*
Go to page 118. 🔊

READING

1 **REMEMBER AND CHECK** Answer the questions.
Then check your answers in the article on page 13 of the Student's Book.

1 What two resolutions has the writer recently made? _____

2 What has the writer done to try and lead a healthier life? _____

3 How is she finding it? _____

4 Why do scientists think we see our 'future self' as being different to our 'present self'? _____

5 How long does our brain need to get used to new habits? _____

2 Read the blog. How do SMART goals get their name?

SMART GOALS

It's that time of the year again that we all look forward to so much. Exams! (I'm using sarcasm here, of course.) Well this year I'm not afraid because this year I'm going to use SMART goals to make sure it all goes well. I read an article about SMART goals. They're what all successful people in life use, apparently.

So what are SMART goals exactly and how are they going to change my life (hopefully)?

Well SMART goals are Specific, Measurable, Attainable, Relevant and Timely. See how they get their names? No? Look at the first letter of each of the words. That's what you call an acronym.

Specific – because they are detailed. It's not good enough to simply say 'I'm going to revise for my exams.' That plan's too general. A specific goal is something like: 'I'm going to spend at least 20 hours revising for each subject and make a timetable to show exactly how I'm going to do this.' That is a Specific goal.

Measurable – because you should be able to measure your goals and ask yourself questions like: 'How much have I done?'; 'How much have I still got to do?'; 'How much time do I still need?'; 'Is this nightmare ever going to end?' Well, maybe the last one isn't such a great example, but you get the idea.

Attainable – because your goal should be something that you can actually do. If your goal is, for example, to raise £1 million for charity, write a novel, climb Mount Everest and revise for your exams then you might want to ask yourself if you really can do all this and then maybe drop one or two of them.

Relevant – because all your little goals should help you work towards your final one. So, for example, a plan to help your mum and dad with all the cooking, washing up and helping out with housework might make you the most popular child in your house but it's not really going to help you with the revision, is it?

Timely – Your goal must have a time frame. In other words, it must have a start and a finish. There's not much point if you're planning to finish revising a couple of weeks after your exams are over. That really doesn't make much sense. Likewise, you need to think about when would be a good time to start. And, as they say, there's no time like the present, I guess it might be a good idea to stop writing about SMART goals and start putting some into action. Goodbye.

3 **Read the blog again. Mark the sentences T (true) or F (false).**

1 The writer enjoys doing exams. ☐

2 The writer is going to use SMART goals to help her through her exams. ☐

3 SMART is an example of an acronym. ☐

4 SMART goals encourage people to do more than they can. ☐

5 You should plan a beginning and an end to your SMART goals. ☐

6 You don't need to think about when to start your SMART goals. ☐

4 **Read the goal. Then follow the instructions.**

'My goal this year is to be healthier.'

1 Make this goal more specific.
_____

2 Write down what you can measure about this goal.
_____

3 Write an example of an attainable plan and an unattainable plan for it.
_____

4 Write an example of a relevant and an irrelevant plan for it.
_____

5 Make a time frame for the plan.
_____

5 **Think of a goal you have and write a short paragraph about it. Is it a SMART goal?**

DEVELOPING WRITING

An email about a problem

1 Read the email. Who is …

1 Dave? ....

2 Kev? ....

3 Conner? ....

4 Gina? ....

2 Read the email again and answer the questions.

1 What specific problems does Kev have with Conner?

....

2 <u>Underline</u> the expressions that show you he's not happy with these things.

3 What plans has he made to resolve the situation?

....

....

4 ⃝Circle the language which introduces these plans.

3 What does Kev do in each paragraph? Write a short description.

A *He apologises for not writing and offers some excuses.*

B ....

....

C ....

....

D ....

....

Hi Dave,

A Sorry for not writing back sooner. I wanted to but I've been pretty busy with school work and football. Next week we're in the cup final – very exciting. Here's a photo of us at football training last week. We had just scored a goal! I hope you had a good time in Dubai – write and tell me what you did there.

B I've also been having a few problems at school recently with a new kid called Conner. The teacher asked me to look after him and I was happy to do that. The problem is that he's now decided I'm his best friend. He's always sending me text messages and wanting to hang out with me. I quite like him but if I'm honest I'm getting a bit tired of him following me everywhere. He also gets really jealous of my other friends and says some really mean things about them. Obviously, I'm not very happy about that!

C I know it's not easy moving somewhere new. So I've decided that I'm going to do something to help him (and, of course, help me too). Next week I'm having a welcome party for him so he can get to know some other people better and make more friends. I've also told him about the youth club and I think he's going to join it. The best part of that plan is that I can't go for the next few weeks because of football training so he'll have to hang out with other people. And finally I know Gina wants to meet him so I've given her his number.

D So that's my plan. If none of it works, I'm going to change my phone number! I'll write and let you know how it goes, but only if you write to me soon. Hope you're well.

From Kev

4 Think of a person, real or imaginary, and write down three complaints about him / her. For each problem, think of a way of resolving it.

problem	resolution
1 He's / She's always …	
2 The problem is …	
3 If I'm honest …	

5 Write an email to a friend explaining your problems and what you're going to do about them. Write about 250 words.

CHECKLIST ✓

☐ Introduction
☐ Explanation of problems
☐ Say what you're going to do about them

☐ Say goodbye
☐ Informal email language

LISTENING

1 🔊07 **Listen to Lucy and Carla's conversation and complete the sentences.**

1 Lucy is upset with _____ .

2 Will promised to help her _____ .

3 He arranged to meet her at _____ at her _____ .

4 Lucy wants to study _____ at university.

5 The application needs to be in by _____ .

6 Lucy asks Carla _____ .

7 Carla says she's not good at _____ .

8 Carla is _____ in the afternoon.

2 🔊07 **Listen again. Complete these parts of the conversation.**

1 CARLA What's up, Lucy?
  LUCY It's Will. _____ with him.

2 LUCY I can't believe he let me down.
  CARLA That's typical Will. _____ to do things and then forgetting.

3 CARLA Just text him and arrange another meeting.
  LUCY _____ the application needs to be in this afternoon.

4 LUCY Unless you could lend me a hand?
  CARLA I'd love to but _____ very good at that sort of thing.

DIALOGUE

1 **Put the lines in order to make three short conversations. Write them in the correct spaces.**

1 Making arrangements

A *Are you doing anything after school, Kim?*

B _____

A _____

B _____

2 Talking about future intentions

C *When do you finish school, Ping?*

D _____

C _____

D _____

3 Making personal predictions

E *Do you think you'll have children one day?*

F _____

E _____

F _____

1 I'm going to study medicine at Cambridge University.

2 Two or three.

3 Probably. I hope so.

4 I'd love to, thanks.

5 Ian and I are going swimming. Do you want to come?

6 Next year in July.

7 How many do you think you'll have?

8 And what are you going to do next?

9 No, I've got nothing planned.

PHRASES FOR FLUENCY SB page 19

1 **Put the words in order to make phrases.**

0 silly / be / don't *Don't be silly.*

1 go / we / here _____

2 you're / star / a _____

3 hiding / have / been / where / you _____

   _____ ?

4 start / where / I / shall _____ ?

5 mention / you / now / it _____

2 **Complete the conversations with the expressions in Exercise 1.**

0
A Shall we invite Jim to the game with us?
B *Don't be silly.* _____ He doesn't like football.

1
A You look busy. Have you got a lot to do?
B Busy? _____ I've got exams all week, I've got to organise Sue's birthday, buy her a present …

2
A Can I make you something to eat?
B Thanks. I'm starving. _____ , Julia.

3
A I haven't seen you for weeks, Dave.
   _____
B Nowhere. I've just been really busy.

4
A I know you've got to study for your exams but would you like to come for a quick bike ride?
B Well, I am busy but _____ , it might be a good idea to get out for a while.

5
A Boys, get in here, you're 10 minutes late!
B _____ We're in trouble now.

Reading and Use of English part 1

1 For questions 1–2 read the text below and decide which answer (A, B, C or D) best fits each gap. There is an example at the beginning (0).

Teenage resolutions

According to a recent survey, more than 75% of 16-year-olds **(0)** _____ at least one resolution at the beginning of each New Year. The most popular ones are **(1)** _____ better at school and being nicer to family members. Other common resolutions include spending less time watching TV and giving **(2)** _____ playing computer games altogether.

0	(A) make	B	do	C	form	D	find
1	A studying	B	making	C	revising	D	doing
2	A in	B	over	C	out	D	up

Exam guide: multiple-choice cloze

In a multiple-choice cloze, you read a short text in which eight words have been blanked out. For each of these you have to choose one of four options to correctly complete the space. This question is designed to test your knowledge of vocabulary including idiomatic language, phrasal verbs and prepositions.

- First of all read the text through without worrying too much about the missing words. It's always a good idea to get an understanding of the meaning of the text as a whole.
- Now focus on each gap in turn. Look carefully at the whole sentence that it is in, and especially at the words that come before and after it. Maybe you can guess what the word is without even looking at the options. If you can and your guess is one of the options then this means you've probably got the correct answer.

- If you can't guess the missing word then look at the four options you are given. Place each one in the space and read the sentence to yourself. Which ones sound wrong? Cross these answers out and concentrate on the others. Make your final choice by going for the one that sounds best to you.
- Finally if you really have no idea, then just choose one. Never leave an empty space on your answer sheet.

2 For questions 1–8 read the text below and decide which answer (A, B, C or D) best fits each gap. There is an example at the beginning (0).

Decisions

I'm just about to start my final year at school and I still haven't **(0)** _____ what I want to do when I finish. I come from a family where everyone has gone to university and I think it's probably what my parents expect me to do too. But, of course, it's not **(1)** _____ to them; it's my decision and the problem is I'm not at all sure what I would choose to study there. When my parents went to university it was free. The government paid for them to get a **(2)** _____ . Although both of them went **(3)** _____ to have successful careers, neither of them actually used the subject they studied. These days it's different. To go **(4)** _____ university is going to cost me at least £27,000 and that's only the course **(5)** _____ . I can't afford to study for a degree that I don't **(6)** _____ up using. I need to choose the right course and, as I said before, at this time in my life, I've no idea what that might be. If I'm honest, I'd like to take a few years **(7)** _____ to do some work and maybe travel the world. Perhaps with a little more life experience I'll be able to make a better decision before I **(8)** _____ down and start my career.

0	(A) decided	B	thought	C	settled	D	fixed
1	A in	B	for	C	up	D	out
2	A degree	B	test	C	form	D	diploma
3	A forward	B	on	C	by	D	further
4	A through	B	by	C	from	D	in
5	A price	B	fees	C	fines	D	bill
6	A start	B	finish	C	begin	D	end
7	A over	B	on	C	out	D	more
8	A live	B	settle	C	calm	D	go

2 HARD TIMES

GRAMMAR
Narrative tenses (review) SB page 22

1 ★☆☆ (Circle) the correct form of the verb.

1 He *was / had been* tired because he *had run / had been running*.

2 My mum *was / was being* angry because I *was watching / had been watching* TV all afternoon.

3 My friends *played / had been playing* football for hours when I *arrived / was arriving*.

4 We *had been waiting / were waiting* for the concert to start for half an hour, when they *made / were making* the announcement.

5 My sister *was learning / had been learning* French for six years before she *went / was going* to France.

6 We *swam / had been swimming* for about an hour when it *started / had started* to rain.

2 ★★☆ Complete the sentences with the past simple or past continuous form of the verbs. Then match the sentences to the events.

0 Her car *was driving* (drive) through a tunnel in Paris when it *crashed* (crash).

1 It _____ (sail) across the Atlantic Ocean when it _____ (hit) an iceberg.

2 People _____ (dance) in the streets after they _____ (hear) he was finally free.

3 The world _____ (watch) on TV when Neil Armstrong _____ (step) on the Moon.

4 The crowds _____ (wave) at the president when they _____ (hear) the gunfire.

5 While people in the neighbouring town of Pripyat _____ (sleep), a nuclear reactor _____ (explode).

6 While Amelia Earhart _____ (work) one day, Captain Railey _____ (ask) her to fly to the UK from America.

Events that shook the world

- [ ] Chernobyl disaster (1986)
- [ ] Apollo 11 (1969)
- [ ] John F. Kennedy assassination (1963)
- [0] Death of Diana, Princess of Wales (1997)
- [ ] Freedom for Nelson Mandela (1990)
- [ ] Sinking of the *Titanic* (1912)
- [ ] First woman to fly across the Atlantic (1928)

3 ★★☆ Complete the sentences. Use the past perfect and the past simple once in each sentence.

Yesterday afternoon I had a guitar lesson.

0 When I *had finished* (finish) my guitar lesson, I *walked* (walk) home.

1 We _____ (have) dinner after I _____ (arrive) home.

2 I _____ (do) the washing up after we _____ (eat) dinner.

3 When I _____ (finish) the washing up, I _____ (call) my friend Tina.

4 I _____ (do) my homework after I _____ (speak) to Tina.

5 When I _____ (finish) my homework, I _____ (watch) a film.

4 ★★★ What did you do yesterday? Write similar sentences as in Exercise 3 using the past perfect and the past simple.

1 Yesterday afternoon I _____

_____

2 When _____

_____

3 _____

_____

4 _____

_____

5 _____

_____

would and *used to* SB page 25

5 ★☆☆ **Complete the sentences with verbs from the list.**

go (x2) | have | live | work (x2) | die | get up

In England in the nineteenth century …

1 Many children used to _____ in factories and mills.
2 They used to _____ very early in the morning.
3 They didn't use to _____ to school.
4 They used to _____ very long hours.
5 They didn't use to _____ nice food to eat.
6 They didn't use to _____ on holidays.
7 They didn't use to _____ very long.
8 They used to _____ young.

6 ★★☆ **Complete the sentences about yourself with *used to* or *didn't use to*.**

When I was five, …

1 I _____ go to a different school.
2 My mum _____ wake me up at 7 am.
3 I _____ eat cereal for breakfast.
4 I _____ walk to school.
5 I _____ have a lot of homework.
6 My dad _____ read me a bedtime story every night.

7 ★★★ **Tony is asking Anna about her primary school. Write the questions. Then match the questions to the answers.**

0 Which / school / go / to
   Which school did you use to go to?
1 wear / school uniform
   _____
2 have / a lot of homework
   _____
3 learn / English
   _____
4 learn / any other languages
   _____
5 What / favourite / subject
   _____

a It used to be Maths. ☐
b Yes, I used to learn French. ☐
c Yes, I used to be really good at it. ☐
d I used to go to Middleham Primary School. ☐
e No, I used to wear my regular clothes. ☐
f No, I didn't, our teacher didn't use to give us much. ☐

8 ★★☆ **In three of the sentences you can use *would* or *wouldn't*. Tick them and rewrite them using *would*.**

1 I used to be overweight. ☐
   _____
2 I used to play football every evening after school. ☐
   _____
3 I didn't use to like chocolate but now I do. ☐
   _____
4 I used to eat vegetables with each meal. ☐
   _____
5 I used to be very good at English. ☐
   _____
6 I used to go for a long bike ride every weekend. ☐
   _____

GET IT RIGHT! 👁
used to and *usually*

Learners sometimes confuse *used to* and *usually*. We use *used to* to refer to events which happened regularly in the past.

✓ When I was at college, I **used to** work in a clothes shop.

We use *usually* to refer to events which happen regularly in the present. We do not use *used to* for this.

✓ I **usually** go to the cinema on Wednesdays because it's cheaper.
✗ I ~~used to~~ go to the cinema on Wednesdays because it's cheaper.

Complete the sentences with *used to* or *usually* and the verb in brackets in the correct form: present tense or base form.

0 I *used to live* (live) in a really small village and I really liked it.
1 We _____ (sing) in shows together when we were younger.
2 These days I _____ (go) to bed early.
3 They _____ (watch) TV on Wednesday evenings because that's when their favourite programme is on.
4 Could you give us the 10% discount that we _____ (get) in the past?
5 He is more attractive than he _____ (be).
6 Do you _____ (wear) that funny hat?

VOCABULARY

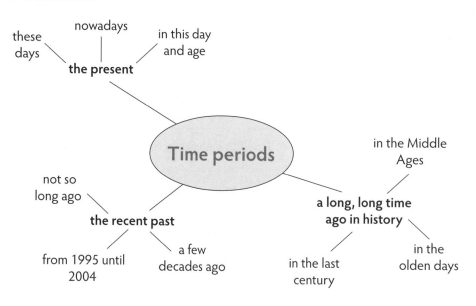

these days

nowadays

in this day and age

the present

Time periods

in the Middle Ages

not so long ago

the recent past

a long, long time ago in history

from 1995 until 2004

a few decades ago

in the last century

in the olden days

Descriptive verbs

dive

flee

rage

scream

demolish

smash

grab

Key words in context

accuse	They **accused** him of lying.
break out	The fire **broke out** just after midnight.
catastrophe	What's happened is a **catastrophe** for the whole country.
disaster	The earthquake was one of the worst **disasters** that ever happened in that area.
elderly	Our neighbour is a kind **elderly** woman.
fight a fire	It was difficult to **fight the fire**. It was so big.
flame	There was a big fire; people could see the **flames** for miles.
fuel	Wood, coal and petrol are different kinds of **fuel**.
household	These days, most **households** have two or three TVs.
lose (one's) life	More than 20 people **lost their lives**, and many were injured.
mattress	There were not enough beds in the house, so they slept on an old **mattress** on the floor.
oxygen	For a fire to start, three things are needed: a spark, fuel and **oxygen**.
spark	A **spark** from a cigarette can easily start a fire.
spread	The wind was strong, so the flames **spread** quickly.
take to court	If you don't pay on time, they might **take you to court**.

Descriptive verbs SB page 22

1 ★☆☆ **Complete the sentences with the words from the list in the correct form.**

~~rage~~ | dive | scream | demolish
grab | flee | smash

0 The fire ___raged___ through the house in minutes.

1 The woman was leaning out of the window. She _____ for help.

2 The man _____ into the river to rescue the boy.

3 The building was unsafe after the fire, so the council _____ it.

4 People _____ from the burning building.

5 The woman _____ her bag before she left the burning building.

6 The man _____ the window to rescue the boy from the fire.

2 ★★☆ **Complete the crossword with synonyms of the underlined words in the sentences. Use descriptive verbs.**

1 Together we <u>ran out of</u> the burning building.

2 The girl <u>broke</u> the bedroom window.

3 'Help me,' she <u>cried out</u>.

4 She <u>quickly took hold of</u> my hand.

5 Later, they <u>decided to destroy</u> the building because it was unsafe.

6 They don't know why the fire <u>started</u>.

7 The fire had been <u>burning</u> for three hours when they finally put it out.

8 People were <u>throwing themselves</u> into the nearby river and swimming across it.

Pronunciation

Initial consonant clusters with /s/
Go to page 118.

3 ★☆☆ **Unscramble the words about fire.**

1 a m e f l _____

2 a r k s p _____

3 g e n y o x _____

4 e u f l _____

5 a s t e r d i s _____

6 a s c a p h t r o t e _____

4 ★★☆ **Complete the sentences about a fire with the correct form of the phrases in the list. Then number the sentences in the order the events happened.**

flames | spread | fight a fire | break out
catastrophe | lose your life

a ☐ The fire brigade worked hard, but sadly three people _____ in the fire.

b [1] It was late at night when the fire ___broke out___.

c ☐ The firemen _____ bravely.

d ☐ The newspapers reported it as a _____ .

e ☐ It was a windy night so the flames _____ quickly before the fire brigade arrived.

f ☐ A man walking his dog saw the _____ and he called the fire brigade.

Time periods SB page 25

5 ★★☆ **Match the two sentence halves.**

1 In this day and age   a not many people had colour TV.

2 A few decades ago   b there were two world wars.

3 In the last century   c there was no electricity.

4 In the Middle Ages   d most people have a smart phone.

6 ★★★ **Write your own sentences using the time phrases.**

1 In this day and age _____

2 A few decades ago _____

3 In the last century _____

4 Nowadays _____

5 Not so long ago _____

6 In the Middle Ages _____

READING

1 REMEMBER AND CHECK **Read the sentences and mark them T (True) or F (False). Then check your answers in the article on page 21 of the Student's Book.**

1 The Great Fire of London started in a butcher's shop. ☐

2 The wind was blowing from the west. ☐

3 The fire started in a wealthy area of the city. ☐

4 Some people escaped by jumping into the river. ☐

5 Luckily, the wind changed direction. ☐

6 A lot of people lost their lives but not many buildings were destroyed. ☐

2 Look at the photo. Which century do you think the girl lived in? How old do you think she is?

3 Now read the autobiography and check your answers.

4 Scan the text and find three more words that show life was hard.

<u>overcrowded</u> _____ _____ _____

My name's Ellen and I grew up in Manchester in the 19th Century at the time of the Industrial Revolution. I was born in 1853, and at that time, Manchester had 108 cotton mills. It was called Cottonopolis.

Life wasn't easy for children in those days, and most children were dead by the age of five. Some might say they were the lucky ones because they didn't have to go to work in a mill.

By 1853, most people had moved from the countryside to the city for work, and the city was dirty and overcrowded. Three or four families often lived in the same house. We lived in one room in the basement of a house. It was damp, dark and cold and we only had one bed. The toilet was outside in the street, and we had to share it with all our neighbours. There wasn't any running water in the house

either. We didn't have any clean drinking water, and many people died from typhoid fever or cholera. My eldest brother died of typhoid two months before I was born. My family had only lived in the city for a year and my mother wanted to move back to the countryside. My father decided they should stay in the city.

I was eight when I started work at the cotton mill. The noise was terrible and the air was filled with white dust from the cotton. I couldn't breathe and I wanted to run away.

The mill was a dangerous place for children. I knew that. On my first day, a little boy died. He was sitting under the machines collecting all the waste when the accident happened. The managers were supposed to stop the machines for cleaning, but they never did. Why should they? Boys like him had very little value.

One morning, after I had been working there for a few months, I had a terrible accident too. I was very tired that morning. I had been working for three hours when, for just a second, I closed my eyes and that's when it happened. A woman grabbed me and pulled me away from the machine, but it was too late, I had lost three fingers on my right hand. At the time I was pleased. 'Now I don't have to work anymore,' I thought. But no, I was wrong. They found me another job – a job where I didn't need a hand.

5 Answer the questions.

1 Why was Manchester called Cottonopolis?

_____

2 How long had the family been living in Manchester when Ellen's brother died?

_____

3 Why did Ellen want to run away when she entered the mill?

_____

4 Where was the little boy working when he had the accident?

_____

5 How long had Ellen been working when she had her accident?

_____

6 What happened to Ellen?

_____

GLOSSARY

Industrial Revolution the period of time during which work began to be done more by machines in factories than by hand at home

mill a factory where particular goods are produced

typhoid an infectious disease spread by dirty water and food

6 Do some internet research about your country. Find the answers to these questions and write a short paragraph.

1 Did children under the age of ten use to work in the 19th Century?

2 What kind of jobs did they use to do?

3 Do they still work in your country today?

4 What kind of jobs do they do now?

DEVELOPING WRITING

A newspaper article

1 Read the outline for writing a newspaper article. Match the information to the headings.

introduction | main body | conclusion | lead sentence | headline

1 _____ This paragraph answers the questions 'what?', 'where?', 'when?' and 'how?'

2 _____ This paragraph (or paragraphs) give more details and background information. Action verbs are used to make the article interesting and more dramatic.

3 _____ This is short and catches the reader's attention.

4 _____ This is usually a memorable sentence to end the article.

5 _____ This is usually a short opening sentence that summarises the article and answers the question 'who?'

2 Now read the article and label it 1–5 for the headings from Exercise 1.

31st AUGUST 1997

Tragedy in Paris

Princess Diana has died after a car crash.

Tragedy struck late last night, as Princess Diana left the Ritz Hotel with Dodi al-Fayed. They were travelling in a car across Paris when at 35 minutes after midnight, the car crashed in the Alma tunnel below the River Seine.

Photographers were chasing the car on motorbikes, and their driver was driving very fast. They crashed into the wall of the tunnel. French radio reported that a spokesperson for the royal family expressed anger with press photographers who relentlessly followed Princess Diana.

Dodi al-Fayed and the driver died at the scene. The Princess and her bodyguard were rushed to hospital in an ambulance in the early hours of Sunday morning. Her bodyguard, Trevor Rees-Jones, survived. Surgeons tried for two hours to save Diana's life but she died at 3 am.

This morning, the world woke up to the shocking news that Princess Diana was dead.

3 Now read the news story again and find the answers to the questions below. Write sentences.

1 Who?

_____

2 What?

_____

3 Where?

_____

4 When?

_____

5 How?

_____

4 Write an article for the school newspaper about a dramatic event in your town. This can be true or something that you make up. Ask yourself the questions in Exercise 3 and use the answers to plan your article. Write about 200 words.

CHECKLIST ✔

- ☐ Use narrative tenses
- ☐ Follow the outline of an article
- ☐ Use action words
- ☐ Check spelling and punctuation

LISTENING

1 🔊 09 **Listen to a conversation about schools in the 19th Century. Which subjects did children use to have to study?** (Circle) **a, b or c.**

a Maths, Reading and Writing **b** Maths, Chemistry and Physics **c** Reading, Writing and Geography

2 🔊 09 **Listen again and match the sentence halves.**

1	Before 1870, only boys	a	playgrounds for boys and girls.
2	After 1870, all children	b	at 5 pm.
3	They used to have separate	c	posters on the walls.
4	They didn't use to have any	d	used to go to school.
5	In the olden days, not many men	e	so they could walk home for lunch.
6	They didn't use to have Geography	f	used to become teachers.
7	They used to finish school	g	aged five to ten used to go to school.
8	They used to have a two-hour lunch break	h	lessons at school.

DIALOGUE

1 **Put the lines in order to make a conversation between father and son.**

☐	DAD	No, the Millennium Bridge didn't use to be here either.
☐	DAD	Yes, it did. It used to be an old power station.
1	DAD	I used to walk along here every afternoon after school.
☐	DAD	It's completely changed. The Globe Theatre didn't use to be here.
☐	DAD	That's the Tate Modern. It's a big modern art gallery.
☐	SON	And what's that huge building over there?
☐	SON	Did it always use to look like that?
☐	SON	Didn't it? What about this bridge?
☐	SON	Lucky you, Dad! Has much changed?

2 **Complete the mini dialogues with the phrases.**

use to watch | your favourite meal
the other children | would play football
in those days | school dinners

1

TINA What did you use to do after school?

DAD I would meet up with _____ in the neighbourhood. If it was raining, we would play board games indoors. If the weather was fine, we _____ in the park.

2

DEAN What kind of programmes did you _____, Grandma?

GRAN I liked films, especially Hollywood musicals. I would watch all the old Fred Astaire and Ginger Rogers films. They weren't in colour though. They were all in black and white _____ .

3

TONY Did you use to take a packed lunch to school, Mum?

MUM No, I didn't. We used to get _____ . The menu was the same every week or every two weeks. I can still remember every single meal.

4

TONY What was _____ ?

MUM I can tell you my least favourite meal – a slice of beef, beetroot and mashed potato.

Speaking part 1

Exam guide: Interview

In the First speaking exam, there will be two examiners and two candidates in the room. You will have a conversation with one of the examiners (the interlocutor). The other examiner (the assessor) will just listen. You will be examined on your ability to talk naturally to the examiner. Part 1 will last for 1½ minutes.

- First the examiner will say:

  Good morning / afternoon / evening.

  My name is … and this is my colleague …

  And your names are?

- Then the examiner will ask you questions from certain categories, such as:

  1 People you know

  2 Things you like

  3 Places you go to

1 Match the questions to the categories above. Write the number.

1 What's your favourite subject at school? Why do you like it? `2`

2 Who are you most like in your family? Tell me about him / her. ☐

3 Do you like reading? What do you like to read? Why? ☐

4 Are there any nice places to go in your town? What are they? What makes them nice? ☐

5 Do you have a best friend? Tell me about him / her. ☐

6 Do you enjoy using the Internet in your free time? Why / Why not? ☐

7 Tell us about a good teacher you've had. ☐

8 Tell us about the things you like doing at the weekend. ☐

9 Where would you like to go for your next holiday? Why would you like to go there? ☐

Exam guide: Interview

- As well as answering the questions you need to give your opinions. For example:

  Do you like reading?

  Yes, I love reading. I've just finished a brilliant horror story called 'Anya's Ghost'.

- Keep your answers short but try to make them interesting.

- Ask the examiner to repeat the question if you need him / her to.

- Don't forget to speak clearly.

2 🔊 10 Now listen to the interview with a candidate. How well did she do? Grade her performance. Give her 1 star for 'could do better', 2 stars for 'good' and 3 stars for 'excellent'.

		★	★★	★★★
1	She gives the correct responses.	★	★★	★★★
2	Her voice is clear.	★	★★	★★★
3	Her word and sentence stress are good.	★	★★	★★★
4	She talks fluently.	★	★★	★★★
5	She uses good vocabulary.	★	★★	★★★
6	She sounds natural.	★	★★	★★★

3 Imagine you are an exam candidate yourself. Answer the questions from Exercise 1 and ask a friend to listen to you and grade your performance.

CONSOLIDATION

LISTENING

1 🔊 11 Listen and (circle) A, B or C.

  1 What does the girl not want to do when she leaves school?
    A make plans
    B start working
    C go to university

  2 The girl says she could work in a factory …
    A if the money is good.
    B for a short time.
    C for a long time.

  3 Why does the girl not want to be like her father?
    A He works evenings and weekends.
    B He doesn't like his job.
    C He doesn't earn much money.

2 🔊 11 Listen again and answer the questions.

  1 Why doesn't the girl want to go to university?

    _____

  2 What does she say about jobs at the moment?

    _____

  3 What kind of job does she want?

    _____

  4 Why does she think working in a factory could be OK?

    _____

  5 What does she think is good about a 9 to 5 job?

    _____

GRAMMAR

3 (Circle) the correct options.

  1 I *go* / *'m going* for a walk in the park every weekend.

  2 Max and I *go* / *are going* for a walk tomorrow morning.

  3 When I arrived, the place was empty – everyone *went* / *had gone* home.

  4 I used to *going* / *go* and play by the river every day.

  5 In the future, life *is being* / *will be* very different from today.

  6 The film finished, so then I *had gone* / *went* to bed.

  7 Tomorrow I *'m meeting* / *meet* my friends in town.

  8 Many years ago, my family *would* / *used to* live in a very small flat.

VOCABULARY

4 Complete the sentences with one word.

  1 In this _____ and age, almost everyone knows how to use a computer.

  2 I've _____ a resolution to never eat chocolate again.

  3 She only started work here last month, but she's already got _____ .

  4 I want to travel – I don't want to get married and settle _____ .

  5 Is this song from the 1970s or the 1980s? Well, it's a song from a few _____ ago, anyway.

  6 He went to university and got a _____ in Mathematics.

  7 The firemen _____ the fire for hours before they managed to put it out.

  8 As you get older, it becomes harder to _____ your ways.

  9 The house was old and dangerous so the city council _____ it.

  10 The post office said it could take _____ to two weeks to deliver the package.

5 Match the sentence halves.

  1 When he reached the age of 63 ☐
  2 The fire broke out because ☐
  3 The flames spread very quickly ☐
  4 When she stopped working, ☐
  5 They were very scared, ☐
  6 She decided to start a career ☐
  7 It isn't a good idea to form ☐
  8 My friend didn't do very ☐
  9 It's up to you. ☐
  10 I was up late. ☐

  a to the next building.
  b well in the exam, unfortunately.
  c in banking.
  d That's why I'm tired.
  e he decided to retire from his job.
  f she took up photography.
  g You decide.
  h bad habits.
  i someone carelessly dropped a cigarette.
  j and they screamed very loudly.

DIALOGUE

6 **Complete the conversation with the phrases in the list.**

don't be silly | where shall I start
now you mention it | you're a star
stuff like that | here we go
where have you been hiding | what's up

JOHNNY Hi, Sophie! I haven't seen you for ages. 1_____ ?

SOPHIE Hi, Johnny. Yes, I'm sorry. I've just had so much to do these days.

JOHNNY Oh 2_____ with the excuses. Like what?

SOPHIE Oh, well, 3_____ ? Like, revising for exams, taking care of my brother …

JOHNNY Your brother? 4_____ with him?

SOPHIE Didn't you hear? He had a pretty bad accident a few weeks ago. He was in hospital for over two weeks. He's home now. I have to look after him in the afternoon when I get back from school.

JOHNNY Wow, Sophie. 5_____ . I don't know how you manage to look after someone who's ill.

SOPHIE Oh, 6_____ . There isn't much to manage really – but he can't move around much so I just have to get food and things, help him get dressed, 7_____ . Anyway, he's my brother so I want to help him. I'm sure you've helped people in your family too.

JOHNNY Well, 8_____ , I helped to look after my dad when he was ill a few years ago.

SOPHIE See? We all do things when we have to. And that's what I'm doing. It is tiring, though.

READING

7 **Read the text and mark the sentences T (true) or F (false).**

Charles Dickens and 'Hard Times'

Charles Dickens was one of the most famous and successful writers in England during the 19th Century. He became very wealthy and once travelled to the USA to give talks. His books are still popular today and many have been made into films – *Great Expectations*, *Oliver Twist* and *A Christmas Carol* are perhaps the best known examples.

But Dickens' life was not always an easy one, especially when he was a small boy. His parents had problems with money, and so in 1824 they sent young Charles, only just turned 12 years old, to work in a factory – he had to stick labels onto bottles full of 'blacking', a polish for cleaning shoes. He was paid six shillings a week – that's about £12.50 a week in today's money. He hated the place.

A short time later, his father was sent to prison because he owed money – this happened to many people at that time. Then the family house was sold, and Charles' mother, brothers and sisters went to live in the prison too. Charles never forgot this period of his life. As an adult, he wanted people to know about the terrible conditions that children often had to work in. And when he started writing, his stories were full of people who suffered the things that he had gone through himself. In fact, one of his novels is called *Hard Times*.

1 There are film versions of some of Charles Dickens' novels. ☐

2 Charles' parents sent him to the factory because they needed money. ☐

3 Charles was almost 13 when he went to work in the factory. ☐

4 Charles' work was to polish shoes. ☐

5 Charles went to live in a prison with his family. ☐

6 In his later life, Charles wanted to help improve the situation for children. ☐

WRITING

8 **Write a short paragraph (100–120 words). Imagine you are 12-year-old Charles Dickens, working in the factory. Say what your work is like and how you feel.**

3 | WHAT'S IN A NAME?

GRAMMAR

(don't) have to / ought to / should(n't) / must SB page 32

1 ★☆☆ **Complete the sentences with the phrases in the list.**

go and see it | go to bed so late | buy a hairbrush | wear something warmer | be so shy | ask someone

1 You should _____

2 He shouldn't _____

3 I must _____

4 I shouldn't _____

5 We ought to _____

6 We must _____

2 ★★☆ (Circle) **the correct options.**

1 It's a holiday tomorrow. We *have to / don't have to* go to school.

2 Well, it's your party. You *have to / don't have to* invite people you don't like.

3 Coffee isn't free here. You *have to / don't have to* pay for it.

4 Just your surname is OK. You *have to / don't have to* write your full name.

5 Well, those are the rules – you *have to / don't have to* be sixteen to be allowed in.

3 ★★☆ **Complete with *have to / has to / don't have to / doesn't have to.***

TOM Why do I ¹_____ go to bed now? Sally ²_____ , and she's only two years older than me.

DAD That's right. But Sally ³_____ get up at seven o'clock to go to school. You do.

TOM Only because you say so. It only takes me fifteen minutes to get dressed and have breakfast.

MUM But you ⁴_____ have a shower too, remember.

TOM OK, twenty minutes. But I ⁵_____ leave the house until 7.50. So, I could get up at 7.30. And so, I ⁶_____ go to bed now.

MUM All right, but remember – it's me who ⁷_____ deal with you when you're tired and irritable in the morning!

4 ★★★ **Complete using a form of *have to* and a suitable verb.**

1 I'm going to a wedding tomorrow so no T-shirt!
   I _____ a suit and tie.

2 Josh, if you're going skateboarding, you _____ in the park and not go on the road.

3 He can't come out with us tonight – he _____ his baby brother.

4 In some countries you can eat with your hands – you _____ with a knife and fork.

5 Her parents are rich, so she _____ about money.

6 Well if you want better grades, you _____ more.

7 We _____ the dishes – we can put them all in the dishwasher.

8 My sister and I have each got a computer now, so we _____ one any more.

had better (not) SB page 33

5 ★☆☆ **Match the sentence halves.**

1 We mustn't be late, so ☐
2 This food might not be good anymore, so ☐
3 We've already spent a lot of money, so ☐
4 It's probably going to be cold, so ☐
5 My eyes are getting tired, so ☐
6 I didn't really understand that, so ☐
7 I think the water's dirty in that tap, so ☐
8 I hate it when you call me names, so ☐

a I'd better wear a jumper.
b we'd better leave now.
c I'd better read it again.
d we'd better not drink it.
e you'd better throw it away.
f you'd better not do it again.
g we'd better not buy anything else.
h I'd better not look at a screen any more.

6 ★★☆ **Use *'d better / 'd better not* and a verb from the list to complete each sentence.**

apologise | call | eat | study
stay | tell | turn | wear

1 A We've got a test tomorrow.
   B Well, you _____ tonight, then.
2 A My parents get worried if I get home late.
   B OK, we _____ too long at the party, then.
3 A I think he's quite angry about what I said.
   B You _____ , then.
4 A I've got tickets for the concert tonight.
   B Well, you _____ Steve. He couldn't get one so he'd be envious.
5 A I don't feel too well.
   B Well, you _____ any more crisps, then.
6 A Look! That man's fallen over. I think he's ill.
   B We _____ an ambulance right away.
7 A The neighbours are complaining about the noise.
   B Oh, OK. We _____ the music down a bit.
8 A It's a very special party tomorrow night.
   B Yes, I know. We _____ something nice.

can('t) / must(n't) SB page 35

7 ★☆☆ **Complete what each of these signs means. Use *can / can't* or *mustn't* and a verb where necessary.**

1 You _____ turn right.
2 You _____ park here.

3 You _____ go in here.
4 You _____ take photos here.

5 You _____ here.
6 You _____ _____ .

GET IT RIGHT!

Confusion between *could* and *should*

Learners sometimes confuse *could* and *should*.

We use *should* to indicate that it's a good idea or that it's what will happen under normal circumstances. On the other hand, we use *could* to indicate that something may be true or possible.

✓ *If you want, you **could** bring some drinks.*
✗ *If you want, you ~~should~~ bring some drinks.*

Circle the correct modal verb.

0 Two hours ⟨should⟩ / could be enough to do everything. That's how long it normally takes.
1 I would like to ask if I *should* / *could* have another month to finish the project.
2 If you want to get healthier, you *should* / *could* eat balanced meals.
3 On the other hand, there *should* / *could* be risks with that plan.
4 *Should* / *Could* you please consider my application and look at my case?
5 I think that we *should* / *could* choose the route around Lake Frene.
6 Maria did not know whether she *should* / *could* tell the police or not.

VOCABULARY

Making and selling

- an advertisement
- a target market
- a brand
- a chain
- a product
- a consumer
- a manufacturer
- a logo
- an image

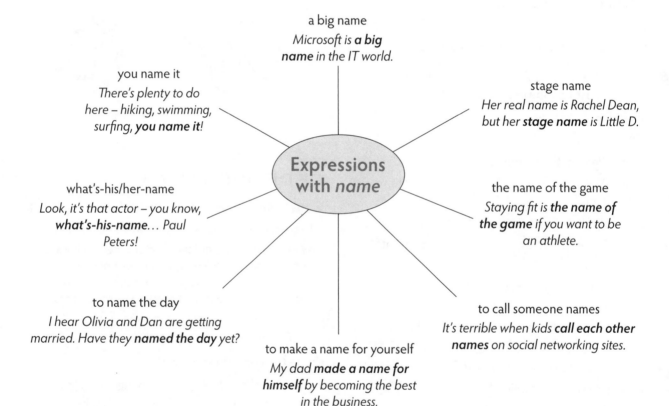

Expressions with *name*

a big name
*Microsoft is **a big name** in the IT world.*

you name it
*There's plenty to do here – hiking, swimming, surfing, **you name it**!*

stage name
*Her real name is Rachel Dean, but her **stage name** is Little D.*

what's-his/her-name
*Look, it's that actor – you know, **what's-his-name**… Paul Peters!*

the name of the game
*Staying fit is **the name of the game** if you want to be an athlete.*

to name the day
*I hear Olivia and Dan are getting married. Have they **named the day** yet?*

to call someone names
*It's terrible when kids **call each other names** on social networking sites.*

to make a name for yourself
*My dad **made a name for himself** by becoming the best in the business.*

Key words in context

approved	The **approved** uniform at our school is grey trousers and a white shirt.
blend in	The colour of the animal's skin helps it to **blend in** with its surroundings.
distinguish	It's important to **distinguish** between work and play.
had better	If we want to pass the exam, I think we**'d better** do some revision.
household name	Prince William is **a household name** in the UK.
impact	She said some wonderful things that had a big **impact** on us.
make a fool of (someone)	I said a really stupid thing – I think I **made a fool of myself**!
memorable	It was a **memorable** day – I'll never forget it.
permission	My mum didn't give me **permission** to use her car.
unique	It's the only one in the world – it's completely **unique**.

Making and selling SB page 32

1 ★★☆ **Complete the phrases with the words in the list.**

product | image | logo | manufacturer | consumer
target market | brand | advertisement | chain

1 a _____ of shops
2 a _____ of things like doors and windows
3 the _____ that a company makes
4 an _____ in a magazine or on TV
5 the _____ that a company tries to sell to
6 the _____ that people prefer to buy
7 the _____ that a company uses to identify itself
8 an _____ that a company shows to the public
9 a _____ who buys goods or services

2 ★★☆ Circle the correct options.

1 This shop is one of a *brand* / *chain* – there are over 30 in this country.
2 I love that company's new TV *logo* / *advertisement*.
3 Some of the best-known car *manufacturers* / *products* are Korean.
4 The marketing department designed a new *image* / *logo* to put on their products.
5 Our company is launching a new *target market* / *product* next week.
6 Many companies support a charity – it improves their *consumer* / *image*.

Pronunciation

Strong and weak forms:
/ɒv/ and /əv/
Go to page 118.

Expressions with *name* SB page 35

3 ★★☆ **Complete with an appropriate expression.**

1 I eat everything – _____ , I'll eat it!
2 Nobody knew him ten years ago, but he soon _____ for himself as an actor.
3 They're engaged to be married but they haven't _____ yet.
4 You've probably never heard of Peter Gene Hernandez, but his _____ is Bruno Mars.
5 Go and talk to that boy – um, _____ , you know, the new guy.
6 Well if you want to play, you have to train too – sorry but that's _____ .
7 It's so childish, I think, when kids at school _____ other kids _____ .
8 Everyone knows who she is – she's a _____ in this country!

4 ★★☆ **Complete the crossword.**

1 → 'Monkey' is not an … name in Denmark.
1 ↓ I want to sell my laptop, so I'm going to put an … in the school magazine.
2 You need your parents' … to go on the school trip.
3 The girl tried to … in with her new friends by listening to the same music as them.
4 It's a very expensive car – the … market is super rich people.
5 I won my first prize today, so it's a … day for me!
6 The company puts its …, a big tick, on all of its shoes.
7 Their advertising had a big … on young people.
8 It's one of a … of 120 shops all over the country.
9 The company is trying to improve its … .
10 This isn't my usual … of toothpaste.
11 All you do is buy things – you're a real …, aren't you?

5 ★★★ **Answer the questions.**

1 What was the most memorable day of your life?

_____

2 What is your favourite brand of clothes? Why?

_____

3 Can you name a song, or film, that has had a big impact on you? What impact did it have?

_____

4 Have you (or anyone you know) got something that is unique? What is it?

_____

5 Who is the biggest name in sport in your country?

_____

6 What is the best chain of shops in your country?

_____

READING

1 REMEMBER AND CHECK Match the phrases from columns A, B and C to make sentences. Then check your answers in the blog entry on page 31 of the Student's Book.

A	B	C
1 Companies really want to find	given to a car	on an English expression.
2 A brand name should be	especially important	and easy to understand.
3 The name 'WhatsApp'	a name for their product	of the whole product package.
4 'Nova' was the name	but it's an important part	that they don't need to change later.
5 Brand names are	unique, easy to remember	that didn't work in Spain.
6 A brand name isn't everything,	is based	for the teenage market.

2 Read the blog quickly. Which of the three titles is the best one?

A People's names aren't easy to remember.

B Why do we sometimes forget people's names?

C Why can't I remember things?

FORUMS   MEMBERS   BLOGS   GALLERY

Hi, Paul here. OK, I'm sure this has happened to you too, right? Last weekend ¹_____ , chatting to some friends, and my friend Hannah introduces me to this girl, who seems nice and starts talking to me. And then some music comes on and I think: 'Wow, this is cool music' and I want to ask the girl to dance – and then I realise I have no idea what her name is. Hannah told me but – it's gone. And I'm too embarrassed to ask her again. So I ²_____ and go somewhere else. Ridiculous, right?

Anyway, this morning I Googled 'remembering names' and there was an article that said that if you don't remember someone's name, ³_____ you don't have a good memory – it's because you don't care. That if you're not motivated to remember, then you won't. Well I'm not so sure. I mean, the girl was nice so I was sort of motivated to remember her name, ⁴_____ . And here's another thing the article said: 'Some people ⁵_____ in their own memories.' They say, 'I'm not good at learning names.' It says people don't remember because they think they're not good at it.

I don't know. What do you guys out there think?

Greg178: No, I disagree. The reason you don't remember people's names is that you're immediately focussed on what they're saying. You don't repeat their name over and over in your head – well, ⁶_____ . Unless, of course, you're more interested in their name than what they have to say.

VVXX: Sounds right to me. Sometimes I meet people and I know I'll never see them again, so I don't even try to remember their name. But if I think a person looks cool or ⁷_____ , then I remember.

JaneGH: It's not that I don't care what a new person's name is, it's just that I'm busy learning other things about them. I'm so busy ⁸_____ their face that I forget to listen for their name. But all I've got to do then is ask them!

---

3 Read the blog again. Put these phrases into the correct places (1–8).

1 but I got distracted
2 don't have much confidence
3 make an excuse
4 taking in
5 it's not because
6 I'm at this party
7 not at a party, anyway
8 might be important

4 Read the blog again. Mark the sentences T (true) or F (false).

1 Paul met a girl called Hannah at a party. ☐
2 Paul found an article about remembering names in a magazine. ☐
3 Paul isn't sure if what the article said is true. ☐
4 Greg178 thinks what someone is saying is more important than their name. ☐
5 VVXX always tries to remember a new person's name. ☐
6 JaneGH concentrates more on someone's face than on their name. ☐

DEVELOPING WRITING

An email about rules

1 Read the email. What does Burcu want to know about?

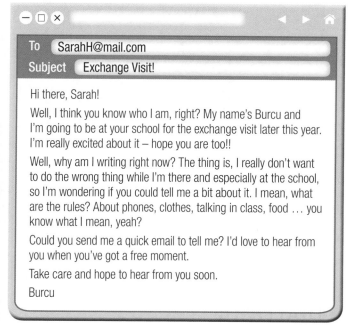

To SarahH@mail.com

Subject Exchange Visit!

Hi there, Sarah!

Well, I think you know who I am, right? My name's Burcu and I'm going to be at your school for the exchange visit later this year. I'm really excited about it – hope you are too!!

Well, why am I writing right now? The thing is, I really don't want to do the wrong thing while I'm there and especially at the school, so I'm wondering if you could tell me a bit about it. I mean, what are the rules? About phones, clothes, talking in class, food … you know what I mean, yeah?

Could you send me a quick email to tell me? I'd love to hear from you when you've got a free moment.

Take care and hope to hear from you soon.

Burcu

2 Now read Sarah's email in reply. Answer the questions that follow it.

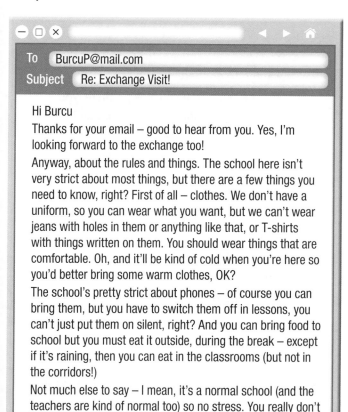

To BurcuP@mail.com

Subject Re: Exchange Visit!

Hi Burcu

Thanks for your email – good to hear from you. Yes, I'm looking forward to the exchange too!

Anyway, about the rules and things. The school here isn't very strict about most things, but there are a few things you need to know, right? First of all – clothes. We don't have a uniform, so you can wear what you want, but we can't wear jeans with holes in them or anything like that, or T-shirts with things written on them. You should wear things that are comfortable. Oh, and it'll be kind of cold when you're here so you'd better bring some warm clothes, OK?

The school's pretty strict about phones – of course you can bring them, but you have to switch them off in lessons, you can't just put them on silent, right? And you can bring food to school but you must eat it outside, during the break – except if it's raining, then you can eat in the classrooms (but not in the corridors!)

Not much else to say – I mean, it's a normal school (and the teachers are kind of normal too) so no stress. You really don't have to worry about anything here.

Hope this helps. Write again soon, OK? And tell me if there's anything else you need to know.

Love,

Sarah

1 Which of the things Burcu asks about does Sarah not mention?

_____

2 What are students not allowed to wear at Sarah's school?

_____

3 What advice does Sarah give Burcu about clothes?

_____

4 What do students have to do with their phones when they go into the classroom?

_____

5 Where are students not allowed to eat at Sarah's school?

_____

3 Answer the questions about Sarah's email. They are all about writing informally.

She writes: 'you'd better bring some warm clothes, OK?'

1 She uses the word 'OK' to
   check for understanding / show disagreement.

2 What word does she sometimes use instead of 'OK'?

_____

She writes: 'it'll be kind of cold when you're here.'

3 'kind of' means *very / a bit.*

4 Find and underline another time when she writes 'kind of' in the email.

She writes: 'good to hear from you.'

5 She has left out the words *This is / It is.*

6 Find two other times when she leaves words out. What are these words?

4 Imagine that Burcu wrote her email to you. Write a reply to her.

a Think about the rules in your school and the things Burcu asks about:

   ● clothes   ● phones
   ● food   ● talking in class

b What other rules (if any) should she know about?

c This is an informal email (like Sarah's) – think about how you can make it easy for Burcu to read.

Write about 200–250 words.

CHECKLIST ✔

- [ ] Include a greeting
- [ ] Use informal language
- [ ] Respond to all questions
- [ ] Sign off the email

LISTENING

1 🔊 **13 Listen to a conversation between Annie, Ben and the new girl. Circle the correct answers.**

1 The new girl's name is …
   A Maureen.   **B** Morgan.   **C** Morwenna.

2 She is from …
   A Cornwall.   **B** Wales.   **C** London.

3 Some places where she's from …
   A have nothing to do there.
   B have names with strange pronunciation.
   C aren't very nice.

2 🔊 **13 Listen again and mark the statements T (true) or F (false).**

1 Annie doesn't understand Morwenna's name. ☐

2 The name 'Morwenna' is Welsh. ☐

3 A part of Morwenna's family lives in Cornwall. ☐

4 Morwenna says Newquay is a good place for surfing. ☐

5 The water in Newquay is warm. ☐

6 Ben pronounces Mousehole correctly. ☐

7 People in Cornwall don't mind if names are pronounced wrongly. ☐

8 Annie gets Morwenna's name wrong. ☐

3 🔊 **13 Listen again. Complete these parts of the conversation.**

1

ANNIE I've never been there. Cornwall, I mean.

MORWENNA Oh, ¹_____ It's really nice. We go quite often – my mum's got family down there. In Penzance.

BEN Anything to do there?

MORWENNA Sure – there are nice beaches and if you like surfing, ²_____ Newquay.

ANNIE But isn't the water really cold?

MORWENNA Well, yes! So if you go surfing, ³_____ a wetsuit, to keep warm in the water.

2

MORWENNA Really. If you go, ⁴_____ how to pronounce the names. Local people don't like it when tourists say the names wrong.

ANNIE I guess not.

BEN I think Annie's right – ⁵_____ a new brain.

MORWENNA Sorry?

BEN Oh, nothing. Listen, ⁶_____ back, the next lesson starts in a few minutes.

DIALOGUE

1 **Put the phrases into the correct places.**

'd better take | should know
should visit | 'd better learn

1

A You live in Vancouver, don't you? I've always wanted to go there.

B That's right. And if you ever go there, you ¹_____ Stanley Park. It's beautiful!

A Is the weather nice there?

B Well, it can be OK in summer – but it rains quite a lot, so you ²_____ an umbrella!

2

A You live in Hamburg, right? I've always wanted to go there.

B Yes, I do. If you come to my city, you should go and see the Miniature Wonderland. It's fantastic.

A Do you think I ³_____ German before I go?

B Well, you ⁴_____ a few words, I guess – but lots of people speak English, so you don't have to worry too much.

2 **Write a dialogue between you and a friend.**

The friend begins:

'You live in (name of your town / city), right? I've always wanted to go there.'

Give the friend some advice about where to go, what to see and what to do.

Use the dialogues in Exercise 1 to help you.

Listening part 1

1 🔊 14 You will hear people talking in four different situations. For questions 1–4, choose the best answer (A, B or C).

1 You hear a man in a shop.
What is the problem with the shoes?
A His wife doesn't like them.
B He doesn't think they're right for him.
C They're too small for him.

2 You hear a girl talking about her hobby, sudoku puzzles.
What does she say about them?
A The puzzles are always easy to do.
B She always solves the puzzles.
C They develop her thinking abilities.

3 You hear a man talking about his trip to China.
Which cities did he visit?
A Beijing, Shanghai and Chengdu
B Beijing, Shanghai and Xi'an
C Beijing, Chengdu and Xi'an

4 You hear a woman talking about getting to and from work.
How does she travel?
A by car
B by plane
C by bus

Exam guide: multiple choice

In part 1 of the First listening exam, you hear eight extracts – they are not connected to each other. You hear each extract twice.

For each extract there is a short statement saying what you're going to hear. Then there is one question. You have to choose the best answer from three options (A, B or C).

- Read the questions and options in advance. It's important to get a clear idea of what you have to decide.
- The first time you hear the monologue, try to remove, if possible, at least one of the answers. Then, the second time you listen, you can concentrate on getting the correct answer.

- The speaker won't always give you a direct answer. Instead, you will have to infer the answer – for example, we can infer 'She is a writer' is the correct answer when we hear 'She spends all day at her computer, typing out her ideas.'
- Remember that you will hear things that are intended to distract you from the correct answer, so avoid making quick decisions.

---

2 🔊 15 You will hear people talking in four different situations. For questions 1–4, choose the best answer (A, B or C).

1 You hear a teenage schoolgirl.
Why did she change schools?
A Her old school was too far away.
B She wanted to work harder.
C The new school is cheaper.

2 You hear part of a radio interview with a man.
What does he do?
A He writes the words for possible songs.
B He is a songwriter and singer.
C He takes pieces of music and writes words for them.

3 You hear a woman talking about her hobby, birdwatching.
How does she feel while she is birdwatching?
A bored
B hopeful
C calm

4 You hear a boy who wants to be a chef.
Why did he first become interested in cooking?
A He ate some good Italian food.
B He enjoyed cooking dinner for himself.
C His mum cooked a fantastic dinner for his birthday.

4 DILEMMAS

GRAMMAR
First and second conditional (review)
SB page 40

1 ★☆☆ Match the sentences with the pictures.

1 If we lose this game, I won't be happy.

2 If we lost this game, I'd be very surprised.

3 If it snows tomorrow, we won't have to go to school.

4 If it snowed here, it would be very strange.

2 ★★☆ Complete the sentences with the verbs in brackets to make first or second conditional sentences.

0 I _will tell_ (tell) you my secret if you ___promise___ (promise) not to tell anyone.

1 Be careful. The cat _____ (bite) you if you _____ (touch) it.

2 If he _____ (be) taller, he _____ (be) a really good basketball player.

3 If I _____ (meet) the President, I _____ (ask) him to do more for the environment.

4 Hurry up. If we _____ (not leave) now, we _____ (miss) the train.

5 If I _____ (know) the answer, I still _____ (not help) you.

6 If we _____ (not stop) talking now, the teacher _____ (get) angry with us.

7 I _____ (run) away if I _____ (see) a tiger in the jungle.

8 Our team is the best. I _____ (be) very surprised if we _____ (not win).

3 ★★☆ Complete the sentences with the verbs in brackets to make second conditional sentences.

What [1]_____ you _____ (do) if you found an envelope full of money in the street? [2]_____ you _____ (take) it to the police station? Or [3]_____ you _____ (keep) it and buy yourself something you really wanted? [4]_____ you _____ (buy) your mum and dad a present? If you [5]_____ (buy) them a present they [6]_____ (want) to know where you got the money from. If you [7]_____ (tell) them the truth maybe they [8]_____ (not be) so happy. And if you [9]_____ (not tell) them the truth, you [10]_____ (feel) really bad. You know what, I hope I never find an envelope full of money in the street!

Time conjunctions SB page 40

4 ★☆☆ Circle the correct words.

1 Dad's going to get a new computer *when / unless* he has enough money.

2 I'll phone you *until / as soon as* she leaves.

3 We'll start the meeting *until / when* Mr Benson arrives.

4 *If / Until* I don't pass my English test, I'll take it again.

5 You won't pass your driving test *if / unless* you practise more.

6 We'll watch the game *as soon as / until* half time.

5 ★★☆ Complete the sentences with *if, unless, until* or *as soon as.*

1 _____ we hurry up, we'll be late for the party.

2 Jim's got the tickets so we'll have to wait _____ he gets there before we can get in.

3 What will you do _____ we don't get any homework this weekend?

4 She can't talk because she's in the shower. She'll call you _____ she gets out.

5 I'm seeing John tonight so I'll ask him _____ I see him.

6 _____ we can't get tickets, we can just watch the game on TV at my house.

7 I've got to go to the shops. Can you look after Tim _____ I get back?

8 I can't go to the party _____ I finish my project by Friday.

wish and *if only* SB page 41

6 ★ ☆ ☆   (Circle) the correct word.

1 My dad wishes he *has / had* more time.

2 Paula wishes she *can / could* go to the game tonight.

3 If only the neighbour's dog *won't / wouldn't* bark all day.

4 The teacher wishes her students *weren't / aren't* so noisy.

5 If only I *am / was* taller.

6 Liam wishes Lucy *will / would* talk to him.

7 If only I *could / can* play the piano.

7 ★★ ☆   Read the sentences. What does Julia wish?

0 'My sister keeps taking my clothes.'

   I wish my sister wouldn't keep taking my clothes.

1 'I don't understand Maths.'

   If only _____

2 'The boys in my class are so childish.'

   I wish _____

3 'I can't find my phone. Where is it?'

   I wish _____

4 'I can't afford to buy those new shoes.'

   If only _____

5 'I want to stay in bed but I've got to get up for school.'

   I wish _____

6 'I've got too much homework this weekend.'

   If only _____

Third conditional (review) SB page 42

8 ★ ☆ ☆   Match the sentence halves.

1 I wouldn't have gone to the concert ☐

2 I would have got a much better mark ☐

3 We would have saved a lot of money ☐

4 She would have got completely lost ☐

5 If you hadn't kicked the ball so hard, ☐

6 If she had apologised, ☐

7 If I had had his number, ☐

8 If they'd been a bit quieter, ☐

a if I'd studied harder.

b if she hadn't had a map.

c it wouldn't have knocked my glasses off.

d I would have phoned him.

e if I had known it was going to be so bad.

f they wouldn't have woken the baby.

g I would have forgiven her.

h if we'd eaten at home.

9 ★★ ☆   Read and complete the sentences with the verbs in brackets. Use either the positive or negative form.

My friend Dave threw a pencil and it hit the teacher. The teacher was angry. Dave didn't say anything. The teacher thought it was me and gave me detention. I went to detention and met a girl called Sara. I asked her over to my place and she said 'yes'. Now Sara's my best friend.

0 If Dave *hadn't thrown* a pencil, it *wouldn't have hit* the teacher. (throw / hit)

1 If he _____ honest, he _____ to detention. (be / go)

2 If I _____ to detention, I _____ Sara. (go / meet)

3 If I _____ Sara, I _____ invite her to my house. (meet / be able to)

4 If she _____ 'no' to my invitation, I _____ at home alone. (say / stay)

5 If she _____ to my place, we _____ best friends. (come / become)

GET IT RIGHT!

would have + past participle

Learners sometimes underuse *would have* + past participle, or use it in the *if*-clause where the past perfect tense is required.

✓ *After the musical, we **would have gone** to a restaurant but we didn't have time.*

✗ *After the musical, we ~~would go~~ to a restaurant but we didn't have time.*

✓ *We would have appreciated it if you **had contacted** us.*

✗ *We would have appreciated it if you ~~would have contacted~~ us.*

Circle the correct tense of the verb.

1 If I *would have to / had to* choose between the two schools, I would choose the larger one.

2 I *would have liked / 'd like* to visit, but I didn't have the chance.

3 It would have been better if there *would have been / had been* more jobs available.

4 The food wasn't as tasty as I *would have liked / 'd like*.

5 If I'd known about the risks, I *wouldn't have taken / wouldn't take* part.

6 We could have learned more if the facilities *would have been / had been* better.

VOCABULARY

Being honest

bad
get away with (something)
hide the truth
tell a lie
cheat

good
do the right thing
be open about (something)
tell the truth
own up (to something)

now

now (for the present)
now that
now and again
just now
now (for near future)

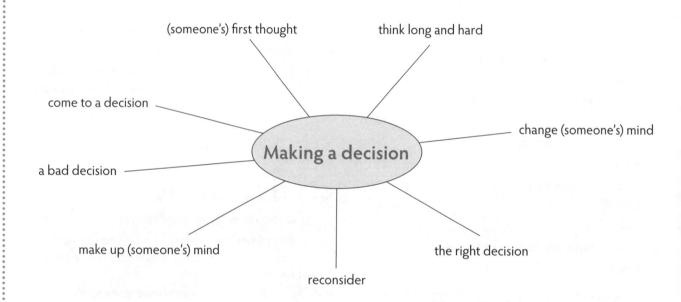

(someone's) first thought   think long and hard

come to a decision   change (someone's) mind

Making a decision

a bad decision

make up (someone's) mind   the right decision

reconsider

Key words in context

as soon as	I'll phone you **as soon as** I know.
go-karting	Many F1 drivers start their careers **go-karting**.
helmet	You should always wear a **helmet** when you cycle to protect your head.
if	**If** you don't slow down, we're going to have an accident.
if only	**If only** I had a better computer. This one is so slow.
race	He won the **race** by more than 30 seconds.
reunite	The twins were separated when they were two years old and only **reunited** 20 years later.
unless	I won't say anything **unless** he asks me.
until	We waited **until** 10 pm and then went home.
when	**When** I got home there was no one there.
wish	It's such a beautiful day I **wish** I didn't have to work.

Being honest SB page 40

1 ★★☆ **Match the sentence halves.**

1 Why don't you just own ☐
2 I want to tell him the ☐
3 I can be very open ☐
4 I always find it really difficult to tell ☐
5 It's not always easy to do ☐
6 There's no point trying to hide ☐
7 She believed me! I never thought I'd get ☐
8 Liam's always trying to cheat ☐

a with my mum. We have a great relationship.
b the truth. People always find out.
c a lie. My face just goes bright red.
d away with that lie.
e in exams. He tries to look at my paper.
f the right thing, so thank you for being honest.
g up and tell her you broke her phone?
h truth but it's just so hard.

2 ★★☆ **Complete the dialogue with the words in the list. There is one extra word.**

truth | open | do | Hide | Own | cheat | lie | get

MANDY So what do you think we should do?
        ¹_____ up and tell the ²_____ ?

RACHEL No way. She'll kill us. I think we have to tell
        a ³_____ and say it wasn't us.

MANDY We'll never ⁴_____ away with it. I think
        we have to ⁵_____ the right thing.

RACHEL Which is?

MANDY Be ⁶_____ about it. Say we were hungry
        and there was nothing else to eat.

RACHEL But it was her birthday cake! She won't
        accept that as an excuse.

MANDY So what do you think we should do?

RACHEL ⁷_____ the truth. Say the dog ate it.

MANDY The dog? That's brilliant! Why didn't you
        suggest that earlier?

Making a decision SB page 43

3 ★★☆ **Match the expressions and the definitions.**

1 first thought ☐
2 to think long and hard ☐
3 to change your mind ☐
4 to reconsider ☐
5 to make up your mind ☐
6 a bad decision ☐

a to really consider something
b to think about your decision again
c to come to a decision
d not the right decision
e to come to a different decision
f original idea

4 ★★★ **Answer the questions.**

1 What were your first thoughts when you met your
best friend?
_____

2 What is the best decision you have ever made?
_____

3 What is the worst decision you have ever made?
_____

4 When do you find it difficult to make up your mind?
_____

5 Can you remember a time when you changed your
mind about something? What was it?
_____

6 What kind of things do you have to think long and
hard about?
_____

WordWise SB page 45

now

5 ★★☆ **Rewrite the sentences with *now* in
the correct place.**

1 I go and see the local team play and again
but I'm not a huge fan.
_____

2 John left just so if you run, you'll catch him.
_____

3 We hardly ever see Lewis that he's got his
own phone.
_____

4 We've missed the bus. What are we going to
do?
_____

READING

1 REMEMBER AND CHECK Put the events in the order that they happened. Then check your answers in the story on page 42 of the Student's Book.

☐ He receives money that helps him change his life.
☐ He remembers advice his grandfather once gave him.
☐ He meets Sarah.
☐ He sees his sisters for the first time in 16 years.

☐ He finds a ring in his cup.
☐ Billy hears a sound that is a little unusual.
☐ He refuses money that would help change his life.
☐ He shows the ring to an expert.
☐ He returns the ring to its rightful owner.

2 Read the article. What was the dilemma the game show contestants faced?

⊖ ⊡ ⊗   **classicquizzes.com**   ◄ ► ⌂

Golden Balls

A few years ago there was a game show on TV in which the contestants faced a really difficult dilemma. I can't really remember what happened in the show, I just remember how it finished. At the end there were two contestants and they had the chance to win some money. Depending on how successful they'd been during the show, the amount of money could be anything from a few hundred pounds to well over £50,000. To get their hands on this money, they had to make one final decision.

In front of each of them were two balls which opened. One had the word 'split' written inside, the other had the word 'steal'. If they wanted to share the money, they chose the 'split' ball. If they wanted to keep all the money for themselves, they chose the 'steal' ball. Each player chose a ball and then they showed it to each other at exactly the same time.

But it wasn't quite so simple. If they both chose the 'split' ball, then they each went home with half the money. If one player chose the 'split' ball while the other chose the 'steal' ball, then the one who'd stolen went home with all the money, leaving the other player with no money at all. However, if they both chose the 'steal' ball, then neither of them got any money at all.

Before they chose the ball, both players had a few minutes to tell the other one what they were going to do.

Of course, they always promised they'd share but they weren't always telling the truth. I remember always feeling really happy when the two players kept their promises and they both went home with some money. It's always good to see the best side of people. But unfortunately it didn't always end that way and when one player stole from the other it made me feel really bad, especially when there was a lot of money involved. However, I think the best feeling I had was when two greedy players both stole. It was great to see the look of disappointment on their faces when they realised they'd both thrown away the money.

The programme showed all sides of human nature, the good and the ugly. It only lasted for a few years and then they stopped making it. I think that was probably a good thing.

⚫ posted 19/07/15   1,425 views   SHARE

---

3 Read the article again and answer the questions.

There are two players, Sam and Jim. There is a total prize money of £10,000.

How much does each player win in the situations below? How does the writer feel watching it?

1 They both choose the 'split' ball.   Sam £_____ Jim £_____ Writer feels _____
2 They both choose the 'steal' ball.   Sam £_____ Jim £_____ Writer feels _____
3 Jim chooses 'split', Sam chooses 'steal'.   Sam £_____ Jim £_____ Writer feels _____
4 Jim chooses 'steal', Sam chooses 'split'.   Sam £_____ Jim £_____ Writer feels _____

4 Imagine you are a contestant in the show. There is £10,000 to win. What would you do and why? Write a short paragraph.

DEVELOPING WRITING

A diary entry about a dilemma

1 Read the diary entry. What is Olivia's dilemma and what does she decide to do?

I have a confession. I've not shown my best friend the trust she deserves and I'm feeling really bad about it. It all started when she asked to borrow my tablet to check her email. Of course, I let her use it. [A] The problem is that she forgot to close it afterwards so when I went online a few hours later, her email page was the first thing I saw. I went to close it down when I noticed an email, a very unusual email. [B] but there it was — an email from my boyfriend to my best friend and the title was my name — 'Olivia!' I thought ¹ _____ . I knew I should just close the page but I had to know: why was he writing to her? I didn't even know he had her email address. I knew it was the ² _____ to do but I opened the message. [C] As soon as I read it I knew I'd made a horrible mistake. The message was all about arranging a surprise party for my birthday at the end of the month.

Now I've got a horrible dilemma. Should I ³ _____ and ⁴ _____ or say nothing and ⁵ _____ from her? If I was braver, I'd tell her what I'd done. [D] I think that this time I won't say anything and pretend that the party is a surprise. But I know there's one thing I'll never do again — I'll never let anyone use my tablet to check their email!

2 Complete the text with the phrases in the list. There is one extra phrase.

long and hard | tell a lie | tell her the truth | own up | wrong thing | hide the truth

3 These sentences have all been removed from the diary entry. Complete them using the verbs in brackets to make second or third conditionals. Then decide in which of the spaces A–D they go.

1 If I _____ (can turn) back time, I _____ (close) the page without taking a look. ☐

2 If I _____ (not see) it, I _____ (never think) of reading any of her messages. ☐

3 If I _____ (tell) her, she _____ (never speak) to me again. ☐

4 If I _____ just _____ (say) 'no', I _____ (not have) this dilemma. ☐

4 Read the dilemmas and then complete the conditional sentences.

1 *I broke my best friend's games console.*

   a If I'd been more careful,

   ---

   b If he knew it was me,

   ---

2 *I saw my best friend cheating in an exam.*

   a If I told the teacher,

   ---

   b If she had studied harder,

   ---

3 *My friend wants to borrow £100 from me. It's all the money I've got.*

   a If I gave it to him and he never paid me back,

   ---

   b If he had been more careful with his money,

   ---

5 Choose one of the dilemmas in Exercise 4 (or think of one of your own) and write a diary entry of about 250 words.

- Explain the dilemma.
- Explain the background behind the dilemma.
- Talk about what you should do.

CHECKLIST ✔

☐ Conditional sentences
☐ Honesty vocabulary
☐ Explanation of dilemma
☐ Background to dilemma
☐ Thoughts about what you should do

LISTENING

1 ◀))16 **Listen to the conversations. Match them with the pictures.**

2 ◀))16 **Listen again and complete these parts of the conversations.**

Conversation 1

TEACHER Is there anything you'd like to tell me?

LIAM I d_____ k_____ w_____ to s_____

TEACHER You know this is a very serious offence.

LIAM I know, Sir. I'm so a_____ .

Conversation 2

WOMAN My dress!

MAN Oh I'm s_____ s_____ .

WOMAN It's OK. It's only water.

MAN I know but it was so clumsy of me.

WOMAN D_____ w_____ a_____ it. Really, it's nothing.

Conversation 3

TINA But I haven't got you a present or even a card. I f_____ a_____ a_____ it.

LUCY No w_____ . It's fine.

DIALOGUE

1 **Put the dialogue in the correct order.**

1	TINA	Tell me it's not your birthday today.
	TINA	It's not fine. I'm going straight out and getting you something nice.
	TINA	But I haven't got you a present or even a card. I feel awful about it.
	TINA	What are you doing?
	TINA	And tonight I'm taking you out for a meal. No argument.
13	TINA	Oh. I see.
	TINA	And I've forgotten it. I'm so embarrassed.
	LUCY	Don't be so silly. It's easily done.
	LUCY	No seriously. You don't need to.
	LUCY	It is. It's the big one – 40.
	LUCY	No worries. It's fine.
	LUCY	But I can't. I've kind of got plans already.
	LUCY	Well, it's just me and a few friends going out dancing.

PHRASES FOR FLUENCY SB page 45

1 **Complete the phrases with the missing vowels.**

1 _r_ y__ __t _f y__r m_nd?

2 b_l__v_ _t _r n_t

3 b_tw__n y__ _nd m_

4 _ w_s w_nd_r_ng _f

5 _ny ch_nc_?

6 wh_t's w_th

2 **Complete the conversations with the phrases from Exercise 1.**

1 A _____ the grumpy face, Ben? Life's not so bad, is it?

  B No, I'm just a bit tired. I didn't get a lot of sleep last night.

2 A I think we should take a break and go and play some tennis.

  B _____ , I was thinking exactly the same thing!

3 A Um, Jen, I don't know if you're busy tonight but _____ you'd like to go to the cinema with me?

  B Like to? I'd love to!

4 A We've got visitors and the living room's a mess. It needs tidying – Jack, _____

  B Sorry, Mum, but I'm busy playing Minecraft.

5 A That dog's really cute. I think we should take it home with us.

  B _____ It probably belongs to someone.

6 A Are you going to Yolanda's party?

  B _____ , I don't really want to go so I think I might make up an excuse and give it a miss.

Pronunciation

Consonant–vowel word linking

Go to page 119. ◀))

Writing part 2

1 Look at the task. <u>Underline</u> the most important information in it.

WE ARE LOOKING FOR STORIES FOR A NEW WEBSITE FOR TEENAGERS.

Your story must start with the following sentence:
I opened the suitcase and could hardly believe my eyes – it was more money than I had ever seen in my life.

Your story must include:
- A decision
- A police officer

Write your story in 140–190 words.

2 Read Alan's answer. What two parts of the question does he fail to answer?

I opened the suitcase and could hardly believe my eyes – it was more money than I had ever seen in my life. I closed it quickly and put the case back onto the seat. I was excited but I was also nervous – very nervous. I sat down next to it and thought about how this case had fallen into my hands.

The woman had seemed normal. We'd started chatting, first about the weather and then about where we were going. She was on her way to visit her aunt. A man dressed in a dark suit passed by our carriage. Her mood changed immediately. She seemed anxious and didn't want to talk. Then she got up suddenly. She asked me to look after the case and left. Two hours later the train had reached its final stop, the station where I was getting off. What was I going to do? Leave the money on the train or take it with me? I counted the money when I got home: £500,000 exactly. I used it to open a small shop. Now, more than twenty years later I have about fifty supermarkets across the whole country. I often think about that woman.

3 Look at the notes Alan made before he wrote his story. Use his story to answer the questions he asked himself.

1 Where was I?

2 Why did I have this suitcase?

3 How did I feel when I saw the money?

4 What did I decide to do?

5 What were the consequences?

Exam guide: writing a story

In part 2 you have to answer one of four questions. You have a choice of an article, a review, an essay, an email/letter or a story. It must be 140–190 words.

- Read the question carefully. Underline the important information. Keep within the word limit. The starting sentence doesn't count in this total.
- Think carefully about who your reader is and why you are writing.
- Use the first sentence given to spark your imagination. Ask yourself questions like *who, why, where* and *what next*.
- Think carefully about what kind of language you will use. When you write a story, you need to show a good use of the narrative tenses.
- Use descriptive language. Think carefully about the verbs, adjectives and adverbs you use.
- Think about how you are going to link the sequence of events. Words like *as soon as, then, after that, before, after,* etc. will help you do this.

4 Read the task. Plan and then write your answer.

WE ARE LOOKING FOR STORIES FOR AN ENGLISH LANGUAGE MAGAZINE FOR TEENAGERS.

Your story must start with the following sentence:
Should I stay or should I go? I had 30 seconds to decide.

Your story must include:
- A dilemma
- A bike

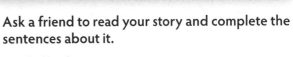

Write your story in 140–190 words.

5 Ask a friend to read your story and complete the sentences about it.

I really like the …

I thought the story was …

The language you used well was …

You could improve it by …

CONSOLIDATION

LISTENING

1 🔊 **19 Listen and (circle) A, B or C.**

1 The girl doesn't want the T-shirt because …
   A it's too big.
   B she doesn't like the colour.
   C she doesn't like the name on it.

2 The girl wants to change the T-shirt for …
   A a belt.
   B a different T-shirt.
   C two other T-shirts.

3 The man suggests that the girl could …
   A keep the T-shirt.
   B give the T-shirt to her brother.
   C give the T-shirt to someone else.

2 🔊 **19 Listen again and mark the sentences T (true) or F (false).**

1 The girl doesn't like clothes with the names of companies on. ☐

2 All the clothes in the shop have the company name on. ☐

3 The T-shirt was a present from the girl's brother. ☐

4 The shirt has a hole in it. ☐

5 The girl hasn't got the receipt. ☐

6 The belt is more expensive than the T-shirt. ☐

7 The girl is bigger than her friend Jenny. ☐

8 She decides to give the T-shirt to her friend. ☐

VOCABULARY

3 Match the sentences.

1 Everyone knows who she is. ☐
2 She's travelled all over the world. ☐
3 She's totally honest. ☐
4 She just doesn't know what to do. ☐
5 She stuck with her original decision. ☐
6 She doesn't want to use her real name. ☐

a She can't make up her mind at all.
b She didn't want to change her mind.
c So she's decided to use a stage name.
d She's a big name in this country.
e I've never heard her tell a lie.
f You name it, she's been there!

4 (Circle) the correct options.

1 I haven't decided yet – I'm going to think long and *hard / strong* about it.

2 We don't go there very often – just *now that / now and again*.

3 Come on, tell us the *lie / truth* about what happened.

4 I know you did it. Come on, you should just *get away with it / own up to it*.

5 I really don't care if people *make me / call me* names.

6 I think you've made the wrong decision. If you want to *reconsider / come to a decision*, please call me.

7 I don't like the *logo / brand* of this company. It's not very well designed.

8 He's the owner of a big *chain / brand* of shops in the north of the country.

GRAMMAR

5 Correct the sentences.

1 I wish you are here.
_____

2 I was happier if the weather was better.
_____

3 If only I know the answer to this question.
_____

4 We'd better to leave now, I think.
_____

5 I'll phone you when I'll get home.
_____

6 Do you think we should asking for some help?
_____

7 He's a great guitar player – if only he can sing better.
_____

8 If he'd left earlier, he hadn't missed the start of the film.
_____

9 The bus ride there is free, so you have to pay for it.
_____

10 Let's wait as soon as 5 pm to call them.
_____

DIALOGUE

6 **Complete the dialogue with the phrases in the list.**

I was wondering | any chance
are you out of your mind | had better
should have been | believe it or not
what's with | between you and me

MANDY Hey, Jim. ¹_____ if you're going to Lucy's party later.

JIM Yeah, I'm going. Why?

MANDY ²_____ I can go with you? I just don't like arriving at parties on my own.

JIM Sure, no problem.

MANDY That's great. Thanks. Hey, you'll never guess what happened to me in a shop this morning.

JIM Tell me. What happened?

MANDY Well, I bought a really cool shirt for the party tonight.
³_____, it was £79.99! I can't believe I spent so much!

JIM Wow, that's really expensive. But so what?

MANDY Well, you know, my parents gave me some money for my birthday, so I paid cash with two £50 notes. I put them on the counter, and,
⁴_____, the woman put the change on top of the notes! I picked it all up and left. So I got the shirt and my money and the change! How cool is that?

JIM Cool? ⁵_____? It's dishonest. Think about the poor shop assistant – she'll probably have to pay that money out of her own pocket. You ⁶_____ take it back and explain. Say it was a mistake.

MANDY No way. She
⁷_____ more careful.

JIM Whatever. I'm sure you wouldn't like it to happen to you.

MANDY Oh come on, Jim.
⁸_____ you?
Don't be so boring.

JIM Boring? Mandy, what you did was stealing, you know?

SPAM

Back in 1937 there was a company in the USA that made a kind of meat that was in a can. The story goes that they had a competition amongst the people who worked there to give this canned meat a name. The winner won $100 for inventing the name: Spam. (Some people think this means 'Specially Processed American Meat). Spam became very popular during World War II in Britain, when it was a very important food item. Spam is still made and sold today around the world.

But interesting things have happened to the name. In the 1970s there was a famous comedy programme on British TV which did a sketch about a café where everything on the menu had Spam in it. They even invented a song which is mainly the word 'Spam' sung over and over again.

Now, when they did this, the comedians created the idea that Spam was everywhere, that you couldn't avoid it and no one really wanted it. And then, more than twenty years later when emails began, people started receiving lots of unwanted emails – they were everywhere and you couldn't avoid them. And what is that kind of email called? Why, spam, of course.

The company that makes Spam (the meat, that is) was not too happy about this use of the name and tried for many years to find a way to stop it. But finally they gave up. Now Spam is both things, and sales of the meat haven't suffered much – in 2007, the seven billionth can of Spam was sold.

READING

7 **Read the online article. Answer the questions.**

1 What is the possible reason for the name 'Spam' for canned meat?

_____

2 When and where was Spam an important food?

_____

3 What idea did the comedy programme create about Spam?

_____

4 Why is unwanted email called 'spam'?

_____

5 How did the meat manufacturer feel about emails being called 'spam'?

_____

6 How many cans of Spam had been sold by 2007?

_____

WRITING

8 **Think of two products you know – one that you like the name of, and one that you don't like the name of. Write a paragraph (100–120 words). Include this information:**

- what the products are and what they do
- what their names are
- why you like / dislike the names (the sound? the meaning of the name? the way the name is written? another reason?)

PRONUNCIATION

UNIT 1
Linking words with *up*

1 Match the sentence halves.

0 I find it difficult to get   `d`

1 I've got too much homework. I spend

2 Hi, Kelly! What's

3 Now that it's winter, why don't you take

4 Last night we stayed

5 We'd like you to come, but it's

6 Have you seen Jim? I wonder what he's

7 She's ninety now and isn't

8 I don't want to move. If it was

9 The test has started. Please pick

a up? You look really sad!

b up your pen and start writing.

c up to me, I'd stay here.

d up early in the morning.

e up to going for long walks.

f up skiing? It's so much fun!

g up to three hours a night doing it.

h up late talking about our holidays.

i up to these days.

j up to you.

2 ◀))05 Listen, check and repeat.

3 Write the phrases with *up* in the column that corresponds to the correct linked sound.

t pronounced	*get up*
d pronounced	
k pronounced	
s pronounced	
z pronounced	

4 ◀))06 Listen, check and repeat.

UNIT 2
Initial consonant clusters with /s/

1 Complete the words with the correct letters. These are all /s/ consonant clusters.

0 I like the top that boy's wearing – the one with black and white ___*str*___ ipes .

1 A _____ong wind was blowing from the east.

2 Her favourite shapes are circles and _____ares.

3 They heard a loud _____ash as the rock fell into the river.

4 She had a headache from looking at the computer _____een all morning.

5 The fire _____ead quickly because of the heat and wind.

6 The people were _____eaming on the roller coaster ride.

2 ◀))08 Listen, check and repeat.

UNIT 3
Strong and weak forms: /ɒv/ and /əv/

1 Match the questions and answers.

0 What do you always buy the same brand **of**?   `c`

1 What are your favourite shoes made **of**?

2 What kinds **of** clothes do you have the most **of**?

3 Do you have a lot **of** gadgets?

4 Which **of** your gadgets do you use the most?

a My mobile phone. Most **of** my friends have one so we text each other a lot.

b They're made **of** leather and they've got rubber soles.

c Chocolate! I love the taste **of** Black & Green.

d I'm quite a casual person. I've got a lot **of** jeans and T-shirts.

e Not really. Most **of** them, like the computer and games console, belong to the whole family.

2 ◀))12 Listen and check.

3 Underline the weak forms and circle the strong forms of the word *of* in the sentences.

4 ◀))12 Listen, check and repeat.

UNIT 4
Consonant–vowel word linking

1 Underline the words where the final consonant is linked to the vowel sound in the next word.

0 I like that film. <u>It's about</u> two friends who go travelling.

1 I didn't find out who wrote the message.

2 My dad doesn't walk to work anymore.

3 Her family lived in Paris before they came to London.

4 They lost everything when their flat burned down.

5 Jenny's mum gets angry when she doesn't tidy her room.

6 Can we have our break now?

7 It was so difficult to make up my mind!

8 His friends felt awful when Tom told them they'd forgotten his birthday.

9 The climb was difficult, so she gave up before she got to the top.

2 🔊17 Listen, check and repeat.

3 Write the phrases with the linked sound in the correct column.

t pronounced	*d* pronounced	*k* pronounced	*s* pronounced	*v* pronounced
			it's about	

4 🔊18 Listen, check and repeat.

GRAMMAR REFERENCE

UNIT 1
Present tenses (review)

To talk about the present, we mostly use the following tenses: present simple, present continuous, present perfect simple and present perfect continuous

1 We use the present simple to talk about facts and give opinions, and to talk about regular habits.

   It **takes** around four minutes to boil an egg. (fact)
   I **think** this is awful. (opinion)
   I usually **go** to bed around 11 o'clock. (habit)

2 We use the present continuous to talk about what's happening at or around the time of speaking.

   What **are** you **doing**?
   A TV company **is making** a programme about life plans.

3 We use the present perfect simple to talk about past actions and experiences but without saying exactly when. This tense links the present and the past and we often use it when a past event has an effect on the present.

   She**'s read** lots of articles about this and she**'s learned** a lot.
   The storm **has caused** a lot of flooding in the town.

4 We use the present perfect continuous to talk about actions that started in the past and are still happening.

   I**'ve been trying** to get fitter for several weeks now.

Future tenses (review)

To talk about the future, we mostly use the following tenses: present continuous, will / won't (do) and going to (do)

1 We often use the present continuous to talk about future plans and arrangements.

   I**'m having** a guitar lesson tomorrow morning.

2 We often use will / won't (do) to make predictions.

   She's very clever – I'm sure she**'ll do** really well at university
   This is the dry time of year – it **won't rain** again until September.

3 We often use going to (do) to talk about intentions.

   Next year, I**'m going to start** university.
   Where **are** you **going to** go on holiday next year?

UNIT 2
Narrative tenses (review)

To talk about the past and to tell narratives, we mostly use the following tenses: past simple, past continuous, past perfect simple and past perfect continuous

1 We use the past simple to talk about actions that happened at one moment in the past, or were true at one time in the past.

   I **fell** over.
   People **didn't have** easy lives two hundred years ago.

2 We use the past continuous to describe ongoing actions or situations around a time in the past.

   I **was running** really fast (and I fell over).
   Thousands of people **were living** in very enclosed spaces.

   We also use the past continuous to talk about an ongoing action that was interrupted by another.

   The fire started while people **were sleeping**.

3 We use the past perfect to describe an event that happened before another.

   The weather **had been** very hot when the fire broke out.
   When we arrived, the film **had** already **started**.

4 We use the past perfect continuous to talk about ongoing actions that began before another action in the past.

   When I finished the race I was exhausted because I**'d been running** for more than two hours.
   He couldn't answer the teacher's question because he **hadn't been listening**.

would and used to

1 We use the expression used to + verb to talk about habits and customs in the past that are no longer true.

   My dad **used to play football**. (= My dad played football in the past but he doesn't any more.)
   When I was a kid, I **used to listen** to pop music. (= That was my habit but I don't do this any more.)

2 It is also possible to use *would* + verb to talk about habits and customs in the past.

*My mum **would cook** chicken every Sunday. (= This was a custom of my mum's.)*
*At school, I **would** always **ask** the teacher questions. (= This was a habit of mine when I was a schoolchild.)*

3 The difference between *used to* and *would* is that we can only use *would* for repeated actions – we cannot use it for a permanent state or situation.

*He **used to be** a police officer. (A permanent state)*
*When I was little, I **used to play** in the garden a lot. (A repeated action)*

UNIT 3

(don't) have to / ought to / should(n't) / must

1 We use *have to* to say 'this is important or necessary'. We use *must* to say that we, or other people, have an obligation to do something.

*Our train leaves at 7 o'clock, so I **have to get up** early.*
*I **must save** some money for mum's birthday present.*
*You **must try** to work harder, Jack.*

2 We use *don't have to* to say this is NOT important or necessary.

*You **don't have to come** with us if you don't want to.*

3 We use *should* or *ought to* to tell someone that something is a good idea.

*At the beach you **should put** some sun cream on.*
*That wasn't a nice thing to say – you **ought to say** sorry.*

Remember: *ought to* isn't as frequent as *should*. It is used mostly in writing, and the negative form is rare.

4 We use *shouldn't* to tell someone that something is not a good idea.

*You **shouldn't spend** so much on clothes.*

had ('d) better (not)

We use *had / 'd better (not)* to advise or warn people in strong terms. It is used to tell people about negative results in the future if they do / don't do something.

The form is always past (*had*) and it is often shortened to *'d*.

*You**'d better** hurry up (or you'll miss the train).*
*He**'d better not** say that again (or I will be very angry).*

can('t) / must(n't)

1 When we want to talk or ask about permission, we often use the modal verb *can / can't*.

*You **can go** to the party but you **can't stay** late.*
***Can** I **borrow** your phone to make a call?*

2 To say what isn't allowed, we use *can't* or *mustn't*.

*You **can't park** here. (This is a fact / rule.)*
*You **mustn't leave** your things on the floor! (The speaker isn't allowing something.)*

UNIT 4

First and second conditional (review)

1 We use the first conditional to talk about real situations and their consequences. It consists of two clauses. The *if* + present simple clause introduces the possible situation or condition. The *will / won't* clause gives the result or consequence.

*If you **leave** that door open, the cat **will get** out.*
*If we **don't leave** now, we **won't get** to school on time.*

2 We use the second conditional to talk about hypothetical or very unlikely situations and their (imaginary) consequences. It consists of two clauses. The *if* + past simple clause introduces the hypothetical situation. The *would* clause gives the imagined result or consequence.

*If I **had** a cat, I**'d call** it Max. (I don't have a cat.)*
*If we **didn't have** a cat, we **wouldn't have to** spend money on cat food. (We have a cat and we need to spend money on cat food.)*

Time conjunctions

We can join ideas about future actions or situations using words like: *if, unless, until, when, as soon as*

When we use these words, we use them with the present simple tense (not *will / won't*) even though the clause refers to the future.

*She won't be happy **if** you **forget** her birthday.*
*We'll be late **unless** we **leave** now.*
*I won't stop asking you **until** you **tell** me.*
*They'll be hungry **when** they **get** here.*
*I'll call you **as soon as** I **finish** this work.*

wish and if only

1 We use *wish* or *if only* + past simple to say that we would like a present situation to be different from what it actually is.

*I **wish** I **had** more friends. (I don't have many friends.)*
*My friends **wish** they **were** rich. (They aren't rich.)*

2 We use *wish / if only* + *could* to talk about wanting to have the ability or permission to do something.

*I **wish** I **could** speak Italian.*
***If only** you **could** come with me.*

3 If there is a situation we don't like (for example, someone is doing or always does something that annoys us) we can use *wish / if only* + *would(n't)*.

*I **wish** you **would knock** before coming into my room.*
***If only** he **wouldn't talk** about football all the time!*

Third conditional (review)

We use the third conditional to talk about how things might have been different in the past. The third conditional is formed with *If* + past perfect + *would (not) have* + past participle. The third conditional talks about impossible conditions (because the past cannot be changed).

If I'd been careful, I wouldn't have dropped the camera.
(I wasn't careful, so I dropped the camera.)
If you hadn't woken me up, I would have slept for hours.
(You woke me up so I didn't sleep for hours.)